Encounter *The* Cross

Encounter *The* Cross

Meditations on the
Seven Last Words
of Jesus

DENNIS J. BILLY, CSsR

Liguori
LIGUORI, MISSOURI

Imprimi Potest: Thomas D. Picton, CSsR
Provincial, Denver Province, The Redemptorists

Published by Liguori Publications
1 Liguori Drive, Liguori, Missouri 63057
To order, call 800-325-9521 or visit www.liguori.org.

Library of Congress Cataloging-in-Publication Data
Billy, Dennis J.
    Encounter the cross : meditations on the seven last words of Jesus / Dennis J. Billy.
        p. cm.
    ISBN 978-0-7648-1941-4 (alk. paper)
    1. Jesus Christ—Seven last words—Meditations. I. Title.
BT457.B55 2010
232.96'35—dc22
                                                                    2010022267

Liguori Publications, a nonprofit corporation, is an apostolate of the Redemptorists. To learn more about the Redemptorists, visit Redemptorists.com.

Printed in the United States of America
14 13 12 11 10   5 4 3 2 1
First edition

In honor of
Jesus of Nazareth,
Son of Man,
Son of God

~~~~~~~~~~~~~~~~~~~~

Jesus on the cross! Behold the proof of the love of God!
Behold the final manifestation that he, the Word Incarnate,
makes upon this earth—a manifestation of suffering, indeed,
but, still more, a manifestation of love!

SAINT ALPHONSUS LIGUORI

Contents

The Cross

Had there been no cross,
Christ could not have been crucified.
Had there been no cross,
life itself could not have been nailed to the tree.
And if life had not been nailed to it,
there would be no streams of immortality
pouring from Christ's side,
blood and water for the world's cleansing.
The legal bond of our sin would not be canceled,
we should not have obtained our freedom,
we should not have enjoyed the fruit of the tree of life
and the gates of paradise would not stand open.
Had there been no cross,
death would not have been trodden underfoot,
nor hell despoiled.

—SAINT ANDREW OF CRETE

Introduction

A YOUNG WIFE AND MOTHER approaches death. She is about to succumb to the awful cancer that has been eating away at her for years. Sensing the end, she says in a low, gasping whisper to her entire family gathered around her deathbed, "I love you all." With those words, she then slowly and gently fades into a coma from which she will never recover. Although she would speak to her family no more, they will remember her words of love for years to come. Through her final words to them, she speaks to her family every day.

Human societies have often found great solace in the final words of their loved ones. As a person nears his or her final hour and is about to cross the threshold of death, whatever is said is listened to with special reverence and is often considered by those around as a final testament about the meaning of life. By remembering their final words, those we love come closer to us. By pondering their last utterances, we are able to share in their life and death, and their spirits are somehow resurrected in our hearts.

This book presents and reflects upon the last words of Jesus of Nazareth as he hung from the cross. It is in keeping with the long-standing devotional practice of "The Seven Last Words," which has deep roots in the traditional Catholic observance of Good Friday.

Jesus' last utterances are garnered from the passion narratives of the Gospels of Luke (Luke 23:34, 43, 46), John (John 19:26–27, 28, 30), and Matthew (Matthew 27:46).

Although there is no way of determining their actual chronological sequence, and even though the historical authenticity of some has been brought into question, the Catholic faithful have listened to these words for centuries and allowed them to penetrate their hearts.

In doing so, they have let the death of their Lord touch them in a very deep and personal way. By meditating on the dying words of the Word-made-flesh, believers of all times and places have been able to enter into his suffering and find meaning in their own.

Jesus' final testament to them has given them the courage to face their own trials and impending death. It has also taught them that to be fully human—both in life and in death—they must personally encounter Jesus, the God of love, and allow him to dwell in their hearts and in their midst.

Jesus' final utterances, however, can be fully understood only in the context of the details of his horrible death by crucifixion. This form of capital punishment is particularly brutal. It was widespread in ancient times and was practiced with special abandon by the Romans on the peoples they subjugated.

Condemned Roman citizens, by contrast, were dispatched through the swifter and less painful method of decapitation.

The purpose of crucifixion was twofold: first to punish the criminal by means of a slow, painful death, and second to set an example so that others would not transgress the law. The Romans made sure they taught these lessons.

Crucifixion by the Romans took place publicly and in the open air. It began with stripping the criminal and scourging him at the place of judgment. To shame him before the people, he was then forced to carry the cross-beam of the cross naked through the streets to the place of execution.

Along the way, he was mocked and often spat upon by those who lined the streets. If his strength appeared to wane, someone was forced to carry the cross-beam for him so that he would not die before he reached the place of execution.

Once there, the naked criminal was fastened to the cross-beam by rope or by nail. He was then hoisted high in the air so the cross-beam could rest either at the top of the vertical beam, which was either permanently in place or in a specially carved notch near the top.

Above his head was placed an inscription listing the crime for which he was being executed. To augment his torments, the criminal's feet were usually fastened or nailed to a wooden support so he would be able to breathe by pulling up with his arms and pushing down with his legs. If the legs were left dangling in the air, death would come much sooner.

When the Romans wanted to teach the people a special lesson, they raised the criminal very high in the air so more would be able to see him.

Death often took days. If the Romans were in a rush, they would hasten death by either breaking the criminal's legs or by piercing his side with a lance. The body would be left on the cross to rot. If it was close to the ground, it could even be torn apart and eaten by wild animals.

With a few notable exceptions, the accounts of Jesus' death closely resemble this routine pattern of Roman execution.

The Jews were given certain concessions by the Romans for executions taking place in Palestine. Jesus, for example, was given back his clothing after being scourged because of objections about driving a criminal naked through the streets (Mark 15:20, Matthew 27:31).

In another concession to the Jews, he was offered some wine drugged with myrrh to numb the pain (Mark 15:23; Matthew 27:34; John 19:29).

Also, his body was not left to rot on the cross, but, in keeping with Jewish law (Deuteronomy 21:23), was taken down and buried before the end of the day (Mark 15:42–47).

Despite these few concessions to the Jews, Jesus' death was horrible and excruciatingly painful. The Romans used crucifixion to break the criminal down physically, emotionally, socially, and even spiritually.

In Jesus' day, it was a brutal reminder of Roman occupation and domination. Compared to crucifixion, stoning, the typical Jewish form of capital punishment, was relatively quick and painless. The Romans used fear to dominate the nations. Crucifixion was a principal tool in their repertoire, one that many feared and that few had the courage to face, let alone endure.

Through Jesus' death, the cross—the symbol par excellence of Roman brutality and domination—was transformed into the distinctive symbol of a new religion. His words from the cross marked the beginning of this important change.

A verse from the prophet Isaiah reads: "They shall beat their swords into plowshares and their spears into pruning hooks" (Isaiah 2:4). Jesus encountered the cross—and embraced it. He responded to the violence of the Roman Empire with the silent message of a kingdom of another world.

Through his death, he took an instrument of death and turned it into a lasting sign of hope and comfort for countless millions. Jesus' last words—all seven of them—represent the testimony of love that would initiate and eventually affect that transformation.

Death by crucifixion was finally outlawed in the Roman Empire by Constantine the Great in 337 A.D., out of reverence for Jesus, the Son of God, and his chosen means for the world's redemption. By that time, the cross had long since been transformed from a symbol of brutality to one of unconditional love and hope for humanity.

Jesus' last words from the cross played an integral role in this passage from death to life. They now have eternal significance and desperately need to be listened to and pondered today by all men, women, and children of good will.

The testament of the Word-made-flesh to humanity speaks of God's forgiveness, peace, and unconditional love. It reminds us of the Father's love for Jesus and of Jesus' love for us. Because of this deep bond of love, the God of Jesus Christ still speaks to the human heart. We need but only listen and allow his words to stake their claim.

Chapter One

Prayer and Forgiveness

"Father, forgive them, they know not what they do."

LUKE 23:34

After all the physical torture, the shame, and public mockery, it is a wonder that Jesus had strength to utter any words at all. Abandoned by many of his closest followers, he hung in ignominy from a cross set in place atop an old quarry known as "Golgotha," the place of the skull.

Because it was outside the city walls, but within walking distance, this small hill just northwest of the city of Jerusalem was sometimes used as a site for dumping refuse. Such was the place of Jesus' execution: his final words were spoken atop a garbage heap.

Common criminals were thought of in this way by Romans and Jews alike. They were outcasts, and the ground upon which their blood was spilled was accursed. Those who gathered under the shadows of their crosses at the moment of execution did so at their own risk.

High atop the cross, however, Jesus refused to curse those who were killing him. Instead, he began to pray and to ask God to forgive them, "Father, forgive them, they know not what they do" (Luke 23:34). Jesus' final words were few, but spoken with every fiber of his being. Each phrase is important and warrants close scrutiny.

"Father." The first word from Jesus' lips as he hung from the cross was to address God as "Abba, Father" (that is, "Papa"). If this had been the only word Jesus uttered from the cross, it would have spoken volumes.

Christians believe that Jesus Christ is the fullness of God's revelation to humanity. One of the most important teachings attributed to Jesus is the revelation of God as "Abba."

Before Jesus' time, Jews typically described the mysterious reality of the God of the covenant in terms of his transcendent glory and almighty power. Yahweh was the Lord of history and the Lord of hosts. He was so holy, in fact, that his name could not be uttered by human lips. To do so would have been considered a sacrilege.

For the Jews of Jesus' day, the distance between Creator and created was so immense that human beings would not dare to tempt him and incur his wrath by mentioning his name. Only special intercessors such as Moses and the prophets could address God and speak to the people on his behalf.

In the temple, God's presence was closely associated with the tablets of the Law kept in the Ark of the Covenant inside the Holy of Holies. Once a year the high priest was permitted to enter this sacred space alone and offer sacrifice in atonement for the sins of the people.

Jesus' death, however, bridged the great chasm separating God and humanity. He is the new Moses, the high priest of the New Covenant, and the sacrificial Lamb of God who takes away the sins of the world.

By addressing God as "Abba," Jesus underscores the importance of the great redemptive action taking place on the cross. By praying to God in such an intimate and personal manner, he opens up a new way for all of us to relate to God.

God is no longer to be thought of as distant and unapproachable but as a loving father who wants to have an intimate relationship with his people. By praying to God as "Abba" and by making this word the first to be uttered from the cross, Jesus celebrates his relationship with God and reminds us we can do the same.

When Jesus' disciples asked him to teach them how to pray, he turned to them and said, "When you pray, say: "'Father, hallowed be your name…'" (Luke 11:2). The "Our Father" is considered the most perfect of all prayers, for it comes from Jesus' own lips. It takes on new meaning for us when we realize that its opening word was spoken by Jesus in his greatest moment of need. Jesus' prayer to the Father reminds us that we should not hesitate to turn to God in our hour of need. Jesus himself asks us to do so and leads us by his own example.

Jesus' first word from the cross reminds us of how he has gifted us with a new way of thinking of and relating to God. It also teaches us something about the very nature of prayer itself. Prayer is nothing more than talking to God. It has to do with conversation, an action that involves speaking and listening.

Although Jesus speaks very few words from the cross, we should not get the impression that he has ever ceased praying. Jesus lived in close communion with the Father, a relationship he nurtured with moments of solitude and deep, heartfelt prayer. Jesus says little from the cross because he spends most of his time listening to the Father in the depths of his heart.

Saint Paul, one of the great apostles of the primitive Church, tells the Christians at the Church of Thessalonica to "pray without ceasing" (1 Thessalonians 5:17). Jesus is the greatest example of one who prays in this manner. He speaks to the Father from his heart, but also listens to him. Most importantly, he communes with him, an action that goes on in the depths of his being and that gives him the strength to give of himself completely, to the point of dying on a cross.

Elsewhere, Paul describes Jesus' death as an action done in obedience to the Father's will (Philippians 2:8). The English word for obedience comes from the Latin word *audire*, meaning "to hear." Jesus understood the Father's will for him, because he listened intently to the still, small voice of God within his heart.

This act of listening ultimately enabled him to speak with authority. The words he spoke from the cross number among his most challenging and penetrating.

"Forgive them." Jesus' death on the cross was an act of selfless giving. Early in his public ministry, he taught his disciples to love their enemies and to pray for their persecutors (Matthew 5:44). The next words from Jesus' lips as he hangs from the cross demonstrate that he lived what he taught—even in death. He asks his Father in heaven to forgive those who are killing him.

For most of us, forgiving someone who has hurt us is very difficult. It usually involves a long, drawn-out process of claiming the hurt, overcoming guilt for whatever role we might have had in causing it, finally recognizing that we have been victimized, reacting to it in righteous anger, and then moving to wholeness and mutual acceptance.

When asked how many times we should forgive our neighbors, Jesus responded, "not seven times, but seventy-seven times" (Matthew 18:22). This startling response demonstrates how central the act of forgiveness was to Jesus' life and mission.

Although not easy to achieve, forgiving becomes less difficult over time. The more we forgive those who have hurt us, the less effort it requires. If we make it a priority in our lives, we gradually find that a deeply rooted attitude has grown within us, one that enables us to face life and all that happens to us with a gentle, forgiving heart. Such an attitude comes not through human effort alone, but in conjunction with God's grace. True forgiveness is a sign of God's presence in our midst. It is a gift from the Lord, one for which all of us should be deeply grateful.

Jesus possessed such a gentle, forgiving heart. His entire life was about healing and forgiving. It came easy for him because he did it so often and because of his deep, intimate union with the Father.

When he asks his Father to forgive his tormentors, he does so from a heart that, within a short while, would be near the side pierced by the lance of one of the very men he is forgiving. By asking his Father to forgive, he teaches us that to hurt another person deliberately and unjustly is also a sin against God himself.

As a result, the person who hurts another in this way ultimately hurts himself or herself in the process. This self-inflicted wound is what Jesus sees when he looks down from the cross and gazes upon his tormentors. Moved with compassion for them, he turns to his Father in heaven and intercedes on their behalf. He does the same for us whenever we injure ourselves in this way. He takes our sins upon himself and pleads our cause.

On another level, Jesus is also asking his Father to forgive all of humanity. His death on the cross was a key moment in the history of salvation. It was a primary means by which death lost its stranglehold over the human race.

In Christian theology, death has traditionally been considered to be one of the consequences of original sin. When we speak of the word "sin" in this context, some of us may raise our eyes in disbelief, because we typically think that the doctrine of original sin requires the literal acceptance of the story of the Fall of Adam and Eve (Genesis 3:1–24). Although few theologians today would accept this account as literal truth, they recognize that the narrative says some important things about the nature of human existence.

Freed from a literal interpretation of the account of the Fall, the classical doctrine of original sin teaches four basic truths: (1) the fundamental goodness of all creation with humanity being created in the image and likeness of God; (2) the need for humanity's redemption; (3) the weakness of creaturely limitation; and (4) the need for the grace of Christ which comes through baptism.

Christ's death on the cross broke the back of the evil called "death" and allowed the process of humanity's healing and divinization to begin. Christ's loving words of forgiveness from the cross teach us that the power of love is stronger than that of death. When selfless love stares death in the eye, it ultimately overcomes it. "God became human," we are told, "so that humanity might become divine." For this to happen, however, death itself had first to be put to death. Such was the price Christ had to pay to effect our redemption.

"They know not." As Jesus looks down from the cross, he mentions the primary cause for all that has happened to him: the scourge of human ignorance.

If only his executioners knew who he was. If only they could delve beneath appearances and look upon him as God looks upon them. If only they could understand that violence begets nothing but fear and hatred. If only they could see what was buried within their hearts and allow their deeper intuitions about life to guide them. If only they could listen to his message without allowing their biases and inner prejudices to get in the way.

Jesus died the brutal death of a criminal because those in charge used their power not on behalf of truth and justice, but to defend the status quo. Jesus, in response, met power with powerlessness; violence, hatred, domination, and oppression with the rule of love.

He loved those who were killing him because he recognized that they did not realize what they were doing. As he gazed on them from atop the cross, he looked with compassion at all who allowed their mind's better judgment to be overcome by dark, unruly emotions. He chose to follow not the path of human arrogance, but the way of the cross. He bids his followers, even those who deserted him in his greatest hour of need, to do the same.

As with death, Christian theology traditionally understands human ignorance as a consequence of "original sin." As mentioned previously, this doctrine (perhaps better termed "the sin of human origins") attempts to map out what is lacking in the human situation.

Among other things, it asserts that human existence, as we presently experience it, is seriously wanting in knowledge. The ignorance it refers to is not the scientific "know-how" that has brought so much good (and evil) to the world we live in, but a fundamental discord between the human mind and heart.

Humanity suffers not from a lack of technical knowledge, but from a lack of wisdom. Within our hearts, we have a sense of a deeper knowledge of reality that should be there, but which has somehow been lost. We are at a loss to explain why it is missing but are resolute in our belief that it was once in our possession. We say this because, in moments of solitude and quiet reflection, many of us are given small, subtle glimpses of its remnants within us. These small traces give us hope that not all is lost. We yearn to overcome our lack of awareness, and we see in Jesus someone who has given us the opportunity to retrieve that precious treasure buried deep within our hearts.

Jesus, became one of us to make right what had gone awry in the human situation. In doing so, he took the risk of being misunderstood by the very people he came to help.

He was killed by our ignorance of our own lack of awareness, a process which, had he not come, would have continued unabated until even those small traces of wisdom within us would be lost. Jesus' death on the cross reversed that process irrevocably. He utters his words from the cross both to the Father and to humanity, both to God and to man.

Jesus, the God-man, offers his words to anyone who will listen. For those who do, something slowly awakens inside of them. They experience the love of God in their hearts and become spiritually alive. Jesus is the love of the Father, and wisdom is the height of that love. Jesus' love for humanity imparts to it a deeper sense of what truly matters. We were born to be in touch with and guided by the Wisdom of God. Jesus came to tell us so and make it happen.

"*What they do.*" After focusing on human ignorance, Jesus then turns to human action itself. He has asked his Father to forgive the actions of his persecutors because of their deep lack of awareness.

Ignorance excuses, however, only when we do not have the responsibility to know. All of humanity, however, had the responsibility to listen to and recognize the wisdom of the Word-made-flesh. Jesus begs his Father to forgive his persecutors even though they should have recognized who he was and were responsible for doing so.

Human existence and human action are closely interrelated. Our actions shape us into the kind of persons we are and will become. Our knowledge (or lack thereof) is an important factor in helping us to decide what we will do and not do in a particular situation.

Nevertheless, ignorance, even when it is complete and morally inculpable, does not alter the external effects of our actions. Regardless of what they thought of it at the time, and putting aside for the moment any assignment of blame, the Roman executioners *put to death the Son of God.*

Their lack of awareness cannot alter the events of Good Friday. Jesus was unjustly accused, tried, and executed. He died an innocent man, and those who contributed to his death, whether they like it or not, have blood on their hands.

Jesus' words from the cross confirm his innocence. If anyone had the right to speak out against the injustice against him, he did. Yet he chose not to do so. His words reveal a man of courage who waived his right to lament his misfortune in favor of something greater, a vision of what all of humanity (even his murderers) might one day become.

Jesus knew what he was doing. He faced the brutality of the cross and freely embraced it. He did so not because he wanted to die, but because he wanted humanity to live and be transformed. He knew that human ignorance—when met with words of compassion, love, and forgiveness—would be overcome. He knew that humanity would eventually recognize the truth of his words and its need to follow them.

Do any of us really know what we are doing? Many of us go through life without being fully conscious of the consequences of our actions. We act before reflecting on what we are doing and fail to realize how those actions affect us.

Much less do we recognize the effect our actions have on others. Jesus was just the opposite. He reflected upon the consequences of both his words and his actions. He thought of the way they would influence others. He chose the path that would heal others of their wounds and bring them closer to both God and to each other. He spoke and acted from his heart, even as his murderers mocked him, even as he hung dying on the cross.

Jesus knew what his executioners were doing. He knew their degree of awareness and responsibility. He knew that he was not the only person being put to death that day. He knew they were in a hurry to get it over with before sunset. He knew that they did not have a clue about what was really going on. He also knew of his intimate communion with the Father and that only quiet tears and a forgiving heart would be an adequate response to such hatred and violence.

Conclusion

"Father, forgive them, they know not what they do."

Although each phrase of this sentence offers much to reflect upon, their combined effect presents a truly unique testimony of Jesus' love for humanity.

In his first words from the cross, Jesus turns to his Father in prayer and intercedes for us on our behalf. He does so to ask the Lord for something that we were unable to ask for ourselves. Because of our ignorance and our inability to accept responsibility for our own actions, Jesus gathers us into his heart and presents our plea to the Father. He stands in our place and closely aligns our destiny with his. In doing so, he makes us members of his body and allows his dying words spoken from the cross to resound deep within us.

Someone once said, "There is a cross in God before the wood is seen on Calvary." It is also true to say that, with Jesus' words from the cross, the cross in God is firmly planted within our hearts. Through these first words from the cross, Jesus reminds us of the intimate relationship that he shares with the Father and offers that relationship to us.

Jesus seeks forgiveness for us because we do not know what to look for or how to go about it. His dying becomes our dying; his search, our search. As he hangs from his cross, his words touch us in a way we never would have thought possible—and his actions even more. Jesus is dying for us. From now on, everything has changed. We look to him to show us the way.

Reflection Questions

1. Do you talk to God? How do you address him? What image or images come to mind when you think of him? Do you feel the need to change your image of God? Do you feel comfortable addressing him as "Abba, Father?" If not, why not?

2. Do you forgive others? Do you find it easy or difficult to forgive them? Do you have to go through a number of steps or stages when you forgive? If so, can you identify what they are? Do you find it more difficult to forgive your friends or those you do not get along with?

3. Do you find it difficult receiving forgiveness from others? Is it more difficult to receive forgiveness from your friends or from those you do not get along with? Do you find it difficult receiving forgiveness from God? Do you find it difficult to forgive yourself?

4. Are you patient with the ignorance of others? How do you react to it? Can you think of concrete examples when you have not been able to put up with someone's lack of knowledge? Are you able to forgive someone who has hurt you through ignorance or lack of knowledge? Can you do so even when he or she is culpable for it?

5. How much do we need to know before we can act? Is it possible for anyone to comprehend the full ramifications of his or her actions? Do you? Do you consider it reckless to act before considering the consequences of your actions? Is it necessary to do so at times? Do you learn from your mistakes? Do you forgive others for their mistakes? Do you forgive yourself for your mistakes?

Prayer

~~~~~~~~~~

LORD, I can easily imagine myself in the place of your executioners. What they did to you, I do to you time and time again through my ignorance and lack of awareness. Through my lack of faith, I have mocked and spat upon you. Through my spiritual and moral failures, I have scourged you and crowned you with thorns. Through my irresponsibility and lack of love I have nailed you to the cross and pierced your side. Forgive me, Lord, for all the times I have hurt you. Help me turn to you and seek forgiveness. Help me to accept your forgiveness, and help me also to forgive myself. Help me to forgive others, Lord, as you have forgiven them. Help me to make your words of forgiveness my own. Mary, my Mother, pray for me and help me never to lose hope.

Chapter Two

Conversion and the Kingdom of God

"Amen, I say to you, today you will be with me in paradise."

LUKE 23:43

Jesus did not die alone on Good Friday. The Gospels tell us he was crucified between two insurgents (Mark 15:27; Luke 23:32; John 19:18). Luke fills out the picture for us to make a poignant point about the meaning of conversion. One of the criminals hanging next to Jesus blasphemes him, saying, "Are you not the Messiah? Save yourself and us" (Luke 23:39).

Perhaps he was echoing the Roman soldiers who just moments earlier had made fun of Jesus, saying, "If you are the king of the Jews, save yourself" (Luke 23:37). The other criminal, however, is sensitive to Jesus' plight. In the midst of these taunts, he turns to the other criminal and says: "Have you no fear of God, for you are subject to the same condemnation? And indeed, we have been condemned justly, for the sentence we received corresponds to our crimes, but this man has done nothing criminal" (Luke 23:40–41). He then turns to Jesus and says, "Jesus, remember me when you come into your kingdom" (Luke 23:42). Jesus says in response, "Amen, I say to you, today you will be with me in paradise" (Luke 23:43).

During the great drama of Christ's crucifixion, Luke presents us with the added motif of fundamental conversion. The "good thief," as he is often called, is horrified by the treatment the soldiers and his fellow criminal give to Jesus. He acknowledges his own deserved punishment but cannot accept the mockery, torture, and killing of an innocent man. Filled with remorse, he turns to Jesus and humbly asks to be remembered when he enters his kingdom. His words to Jesus reveal both a change of heart and the life-giving act of faith. How fitting it is that someone should come to believe at the very hour of Jesus' death. Jesus' words have great relevance and, once again, warrant close scrutiny.

"Amen, I say to you." Jesus' first words to the thief are designed to give him confidence. No one knows with certainty what lies beyond the pale of death. Most of us think about it only when we are forced into it. Such was probably the case of the two criminals on either side of Jesus: one mocks Jesus while, at the same time, trying to find a way of escaping death ("save yourself *and us*); the other is preparing to meet his death and, in doing so, is looking to what lies beyond it ("*remember me* when you come into your kingdom").

Because they are facing the darkest moment of their lives, it is probably fair to conclude that both men are afraid. Jesus responds to one with silence and to the other with a word of assurance. His silence to the first criminal is in keeping with his refusal to defend himself throughout his ordeal. If the first criminal encounters himself in this silence, he will probably get in touch with his fear and begin to think about facing his death rather than escaping from it. The good thief, however, is already pondering his imminent death—and even looking beyond it.

After having expressed his sorrow to Jesus, he finds within himself the smallest glimmer of faith. Jesus, in turn, looks at him and gives him a word of assurance to ease his fears: "Amen, I say to you."

Jesus faces his death with courage. His complete and utter trust in his Father's love for him enables him to overcome his fears from the night before (Matthew 26:36–46; Mark 14:32–42; Luke 22:39–46).

His first words to the good thief seek to alleviate whatever fears he might have at his approaching death. In effect, he is telling the good thief to trust in him. Jesus, we know, was someone who spoke with authority (Matthew 7:29; Luke 4:32). Even as he hung from the cross and let out these words of assurance to the thief beside him, we can be sure that they achieved what they were intended for. Jesus' words gave the man confidence and helped him to face death with courage.

The good thief's conversation with Jesus also offers us a good example of the dynamics of the dialogue of Christian prayer. The thief turns to Jesus in his hour of greatest need. With a few heartfelt words, he tells Jesus of his remorse and expresses his deepest hope. Jesus' words, in turn, give him the strength and confidence to face the demands of the hour.

Within a short time, this criminal's legs will be broken and his death hastened. The strength and confidence found in Jesus' words represent the help we receive from God when we share our deepest needs and concerns with him. Authentic prayer does not seek to escape the demands that life has placed before us—be it even death—but to face them with renewed confidence and hope. The good thief's dialogue with Jesus points us in the right direction. It reminds us of the kind of relationship we are called to have with him and also that it is never too late to start.

It also reminds us that confidence in God springs from the bonds we share with him through Christ. No one knows what image of God the good thief had before his conversation with Jesus. One can only hope, however, that, by listening to Jesus and watching him suffer innocently and without complaint, he came to know God at the moment of his death in a way that few, if any, had ever known before.

Jesus reveals the Father to us and presents us to him. He is our intercessor before God, the one who pleads for us on our behalf and who allows us to share an intimacy with the divine that we never before thought possible. He is the one who gives us confidence. He assures us, just as he did the good thief, that when we stare into the face of death at our final moments, there is nothing to fear.

"*Today.*" Jesus' words to the good thief are meant to encourage him in his moment of suffering. He promises the poor criminal something concrete and tangible that is to have almost immediate effect. His words of assurance are not about tomorrow, or next week, or next month, or next year, but about *today:* the day of the good thief's salvation.

Jesus' death by crucifixion was an event that took place both in and out of time. It occurred in time, at a particular moment in history but had eternal significance for all of humanity. When

Jesus spoke to the good thief of "today," he was announcing the nearness of the kingdom.

Just as the eternal Word of God broke through the boundaries of time and space to become human, so, too, would it break through the boundaries of death to return to the Father. When Jesus entered upon his kingdom, he would take his humanity with him—and all those who shared in it. The good thief numbered among the first to enter.

The kingdom of God has to do with the spread of God's love. It takes root first in our hearts and then through the bonds of love that we share with others.

When Jesus walked this earth, the love of God was visible for all to see. When he died on the cross, the extent of that love was clearly demonstrated.

The good thief witnessed this love firsthand. He was a sinful man who suffered at Jesus' side. Like Jesus, he was stripped and scourged. He, too, had to carry his cross-beam through the streets of Jerusalem, outside the city gates, to the top of Golgotha. He, too, was fastened to the cross and lifted up. Yet, when he looked at Jesus, he saw a big difference. Jesus' innocence and quiet suffering in the face of injustice touched him to the quick.

When Jesus looked to this thief and told him about what was to happen "today," he gave him the opportunity to unite his suffering to his cross of innocent suffering.

In Jesus, the kingdom of God was already present in our midst for all to see. Although it was not of this world, it could take root in this world through anyone who dared open his or her heart to his words.

"Today" was the day of salvation for the good thief, because he opened his heart and united his sufferings to Christ's. "Today" can also be the day of our salvation. For it to happen, all we need to do is open up our own hearts to Christ so that whatever suffering we are experiencing in the present moment can be united to his and hung upon the bleeding cross of innocence. Jesus suffered beside the good thief and welcomed him into his kingdom. "Today" he makes the same offering to us.

Jesus wants to be present to us now, on this very day, regardless of the situation in which we find ourselves. We may think that we are not worthy of God's love because of something we have done. Jesus asks us not to worry. He came to this world to help us let go of our burden.

We may be interested in accepting God's love in our hearts but find ourselves too busy to do so now. Jesus asks us to try to make the time now, before it is too late. The most important thing in the world for any of us is the relationship we have with God.

Unlike the good thief, let us not wait until the final moments of life to receive this precious gift. Today, this day, is the day for turning our hearts to the Lord. Today, this day, is the day for living in the present moment.

Let us not worry about the past or the future. Jesus wants us to enter his kingdom of love today. If we allow it, it will rise within our hearts and pour out from there into our midst. To be a citizen of that kingdom, while actually walking upon the earth, is something the good thief never had an opportunity to do. We have that opportunity and should take advantage of it.

"You will be with me." Jesus then extends words of friendship to the thief, telling him that they will be together after death. In the Gospel of John, Jesus tells his disciples: "No one has greater love than this, to lay down one's life for one's friends." (John 15:13). Jesus looks upon the thief as his friend. In him, he sees the reason

for his suffering. Jesus would have laid down his life in this way even if the thief were the only person in the world. He looks upon each individual in that way. Every one of us is loved by the Lord as if he or she were the only person alive.

True friendship has three characteristics: benevolence, reciprocity, and mutual indwelling. Friends wish each other well and actively seek the other's well-being. Since friendship cannot be forced, friends must do so freely and mutually. Doing so establishes a bond between the two persons that results in a deep sense of sharing in each other's life. Good friends carry each other in their hearts. They are present to one another even when separated by great distances. They commune with one another and long to be in each other's presence.

Jesus befriends the thief and says, "You will be with me." Friends get closer by being present to one another. They do so not necessarily by spending all of their time together (important as it may be), but by thinking about the other's needs and putting them before one's own. They grow in intimacy by giving the other loving attention and heartfelt sharing. Self-disclosure is an important sign of intimacy. Friends cannot draw close if they do not participate in each other's lives. The closer we are to a person, the more of ourselves we are willing to reveal. When we find ourselves pretending or holding something back from someone we love, then something is going wrong in the relationship.

As he hung from his cross, Jesus held nothing back from the good thief. He listened to the poor man's plea. He had compassion for him and extended to him words of encouragement and hope. He also spoke to him of his kingdom and promised him that they would go there together before the day was out. Jesus spoke of things that mattered to him. He opened his heart to the man dying next to him. He was present to him. He communed with him in his hour of need. Within a few short moments, he became his close, intimate friend.

In Jesus' kingdom, everyone is everyone else's close, intimate friend. These friendships are based not on common interests or changing likes and dislikes, but on the love of God. "Charity," we are told, "is a kind of friendship of man for God." To share in the love of God is to share in God's friendship. Those who enjoy this friendship do so not only with God, but also with one another. Jesus expressed this love to the good thief. He also expresses it to us. He looks at us, listens to our problems and concerns—whatever they may be—and tells us that he will be with us and that we will be with each other.

Jesus is present to us and wishes to commune with us. Is he not, after all, "Emmanuel, God...with us" (Matthew 1:23)? Is that not why he gave us his body to eat and his blood to drink? Jesus wishes to dwell within our hearts and wants ever so much for our hearts to dwell in his. He also wants us to dwell in each other's hearts. For both to happen we need only to look to him from where we are and, like the good thief hanging from his cross in his dying moments, ask to be remembered by him as he enters upon his reign.

"In paradise." When Jesus tells the thief hanging at his side that they would soon be together in paradise, he is alluding to what the Jews of the time understood as "the eternal abode of the just." "Paradise" is a word of Persian origin meaning "garden" that eventually found its way into Hebrew and then into Greek. It is the word used to describe the garden of Eden, where God placed Adam and Eve and from whence they were driven after their Fall from grace (see Genesis 2:15; 3:23). Later, it was used to refer to the place where the just went after death to receive their eternal reward. Although its use in Luke's Gospel points to the latter use, it is quite possible that both meanings are intended.

When Jesus speaks of "paradise" to the good thief, he seems to be referring to a state of peace and justice beyond the present world. He himself, after all, stated that his kingdom was not of this world (see John 18:36). There is more here, however, than meets the eye. Jesus' death is not just any death. Along with the incarnation and resurrection, it rests at the very heart of salvation history.

Through his life, death, and resurrection, Jesus redeemed the world. Redemption in this context refers specifically to the recreation of human nature that was made necessary as a result of humanity's Fall from grace.

Saint Paul talks of Jesus as the new Adam: "For just as in Adam all die, so too in Christ shall all be brought to life" (1 Corinthians 15:22). The use of the word "paradise," at this particular moment of Luke's passion narrative seems to be a specific reference to the end of humanity's time of exile.

Just as God drove out sinful man from "paradise," so does he lead him back so that he could once again walk in the presence of God. This paradise is not the garden of Eden of the Genesis account, but a state of being where people are once again able to commune with God.

Communing with God, after all, is what Jesus is all about. He came to this world for one reason: to reconcile the human with the divine. He did this by entering our world, by giving himself completely, by becoming our nourishment and source of hope. He did all this so that we could once again enjoy fellowship with the divine.

Someone once said, "Paradise for God is to dwell in the human heart." When we think of "heaven" or "paradise," we think all too often of the beatific vision and what it would be like to see God face-to-face. We sometimes forget that God in his goodness wishes to pour out his love on all creation.

Humanity is not only God's creation grown to an awareness of itself but also the place where the divine wishes to make its earthly abode. God desires to journey with us through life. He wants to be our companion, our fellow pilgrim. He seeks to do this by dwelling in our hearts. Heaven, for God, is beating within us. He wishes to make our hearts sacred by residing there through his spirit and making it his holy dwelling.

When Jesus speaks of "paradise," the human heart cannot be far from his thoughts. The good thief was closer to it than he thought. It was his inner conversion of heart that turned him toward Jesus and that inspired him to ask to address Jesus.

Moreover, it was Jesus' heart that reached out to him in his moment of agony to encourage him and give him hope. It is your heart and my heart. It is every human heart that turns to Jesus and humbly asks him to be born there, to grow there, to dwell there, and journey with it.

Through Jesus, the distance between the human heart and the heart of God has been bridged. All that remains is for each of us to allow God to walk across and lead us home.

Conclusion

"Amen, I say to you, today you will be with me in paradise."

Jesus' words to the good thief inspire hope and confidence. They remind us that it is never too late to open our hearts to God and seek forgiveness. Without this fundamental conversion of heart, we would not be able to enter the kingdom. Or perhaps it would be better to say that the kingdom would not be able to enter us. "Paradise for God," we must remember, "is to dwell in the human heart."

Not far from the Lateran Basilica, the Cistercian Church of the Holy Cross of Jerusalem houses one of the most fascinating relics in Rome: the cross-beam of the good thief. Putting aside the historical question of the relic's authenticity (a problem that cannot be scientifically resolved), this slender beam of wood invites us to imagine ourselves in Luke's passion narrative.

In a time when few people knew how to read and write, the Church often used artifacts, scenes, and images from the Gospels to build up the faith of the people. They might not be able to read the passion narrative of Luke, but they certainly could listen to it and identify with the various characters, places, and things in it.

Gazing upon this ancient wood, our imagination transports us atop Golgotha and places us on a cross next to our suffering Lord. There beside Jesus, we relive the good thief's conversation with Jesus and are able to enter into one of the narrative's most important themes: our need for conversion.

As Jesus dies for the sins of the world, the good thief turns to him and experiences a change of heart. When looking at the cross, while hanging from our own, we also sense the need for conversion in our lives. The thief's cross and sorrowful plea become our own. We sense Jesus next to us and are inspired to turn to him. He is closer to us that we think. His words bring us comfort, for we sense his love and know that, no matter what happens, he is suffering with us and will be with us this day (and always) in paradise.

Reflection Questions

1. Which of the two thieves do you identify most with? Which would you prefer to be like? Do you ever taunt God as the bad thief taunted Jesus? Do you ever seek forgiveness for your sins from Jesus like the good thief? Do you believe that there is always hope for you, even at the last minute and no matter what you have done?

2. What is your greatest fear? Are you able to verbalize it? Do you know why it causes you to be afraid? Have you ever shared your fear with another person? Have you ever shared it with God? Do you share your innermost fears with God or do you try to hide and keep them from him?

3. What is your attitude toward death? Are you afraid of it? Do you ignore it? Do you try to escape its presence in your life? Do you think you will face death with confidence or with fear and uncertainty? Do you believe in life after death? If so, have you ever wondered what it will be like? If not, what are your reasons for not believing?

4. Do you believe that God has a personal interest in you? Do you think of God as your friend? Do you ever talk to God straight from the heart, like one friend to another? What is preventing you from talking to him in this way now? Do you believe that

God will be with you at the moment of your death? Do you believe he will dwell within your heart and take you to paradise?

5. What is paradise for you? What is paradise for God? Do you see a connection between the two? Does it have anything to do with dwelling in each other's hearts? If so, then can paradise for both you and for God begin before death? Is that what Jesus means when he says that the reign of God is within us? Is that what he means when he says that the reign of God is in our midst?

Prayer

Lord, I can imagine myself as both thieves hanging by your side. Like the bad thief, a part of me wants to taunt you and challenge you to get down from the cross and save yourself. Like the good thief, another side of me looks to you in sorrow, seeking forgiveness for my sins. Convert me, Lord, that I might be converted. Help me to overcome this struggle within me between good and evil. Help me to follow you and turn to you always, especially in my time of need. Remember me in your kingdom, Lord. Reign within my heart and help me to experience paradise. Help me to turn to you at all times, especially at the moment of my death. Help me to converse with you from the heart and to trust what you reveal to me there. Mary, my mother, pray for me.

Chapter Three
The Family of God

*"Woman, behold, your son...
Behold, your mother."*

JOHN 19:26–27

On the day of his death, Jesus' closest disciples abandoned him. Their courage failed them and they ran away out of fear of what the Romans might do to them.

Judas betrayed him; Peter denied him; and most of the other apostles fled. The Gospels give conflicting accounts of who stayed with him during his horrible ordeal. Mark's Gospel says there were women watching from a distance (Mark 15:40). Matthew's Gospel says many women were looking on from a distance (Matthew 27:55). Luke's Gospel says all of his friends and the women who had accompanied him from Galilee were watching him from a distance (Luke 23:49). John's Gospel places the women much closer: "Standing by the cross of Jesus were his mother and his mother's sister, Mary the wife of Clopas, and Mary of Magdala" (John 19:25). This version also has the beloved disciple at the foot of the cross (John 19:26).

Some try to reconcile these accounts by saying that a group of Jesus' followers (mostly women) first looked on from a distance, but then Jesus' mother and a few others moved up closer when she saw her son drawing closer to death.

John's Gospel alone places the beloved disciple at the foot of the cross. The author uses this character elsewhere in his Gospel to say something about the meaning of Christian discipleship. He is most likely doing the same in this instance. If so, then Jesus' words from the cross have special significance for us: "Seeing his mother there with the disciple whom he loved, Jesus said to his mother, 'Woman, behold, your son.' In turn, he said to his disciple, 'Behold, your mother.' From that hour onward, the disciple took her into his care" (John 19:26–27). Each of Jesus' words from the cross once again invites fitting commentary.

"Woman." Jesus' death on the cross was a pivotal moment in the history of salvation. The words he said in his final hours have significance not just for the historical moment in which he uttered them, but for all time. Jesus' words to his mother, Mary, and to the beloved disciple reflect this universal significance. As he looks down upon them from the cross, one gets the sense that he is speaking not only to them but also to us.

Jesus addresses his mother, Mary, as "Woman." It was not typical for Jews to address their mothers in this way. Rather than saying, "Mother," he chooses to address her with a much more common title. Any woman in Roman-occupied Palestine could have been addressed thus (see John 4:21). The term gives no indication that Mary enjoyed any unique relationship to her son. Jesus seems to be saying that relationships in the kingdom of God do not reflect their earthly ties.

Jesus relates to his mother first and foremost as "Woman." That Mary is standing at the foot of the cross next to the beloved disciple has special relevance. For Jesus, relationships in the kingdom are based not on blood ties, but on discipleship and doing the will of God.

In other Gospel stories, Jesus makes his point dramatically clear: "'Who are my mother and (my) brothers?' And looking around him at those seated in the circle, he said, 'Here are my mother and my brothers. (For) whoever does the will of God is my brother and sister and mother'" (Mark 3:33–35).

Even though Mary, through her humble fiat (Luke 1:38), becomes for the community of the faithful the disciple par excellence, Jesus still chooses to speak to her in this way. It is fitting that she is the first woman he addresses as he enters upon his reign. His decision to call her, "Woman," sets up an important parallel with Adam's wife, Eve, from the Genesis account of the Fall (see Genesis 3:1–24). Eve was the first woman to leave paradise; Mary would be the first to be recognized in (and eventually enter) the kingdom of God. Eve participated in humanity's original downfall; Mary participated in a special way in its restoration and final redemption.

Saint Irenaeus of Lyons (c. 180) develops this important parallel between Eve and Mary: "As Eve was seduced by the word of an angel and so fled from God after disobeying his word, Mary in her turn was given the Good News by the word of an angel, and bore God in obedience to his word. As Eve was seduced into disobedience to God, so Mary was persuaded into obedience to God; thus Mary became the advocate of the virgin Eve."

If we examine more deeply the reason why Jesus calls Mary,

"Woman," rather than, "Mother," we see that he also wishes to cast Mary as the great woman foretold in Genesis who would crush the serpent's head: "I will put enmity between you and the woman, and between your offspring and hers; He will strike at your head, while you strike at his heel" (Genesis 3:15).

Mary, Jesus is saying, has played a unique role in the history of salvation. By accepting the will of God in her life and giving birth to Jesus, God's only begotten Son, she brings into the world the one person who can overcome the forces of evil once and for all. The serpent's head will be crushed only because Mary has given birth to the one who would do it. As death entered the world through a woman's help, so would it leave it in this way.

In the light of Mary's unique role in our redemption, a certain passage in the Book of Revelation takes on greater significance. It speaks of "a woman clothed with the sun, with the moon under her feet, and on her head a crown of twelve stars" (Revelation 12:1). This woman is with child and wails aloud in pain as she is about to give birth when a huge, flaming red dragon appears before her ready devour her child. The woman gives birth to a son, and he is destined to shepherd many nations (see Revelation 12:1–5). The woman in this passage has been identified with God's people of both the Old and New Testaments. Since Mary, the mother of Jesus, is the mother of the Church, the new Israel, the passage applies to her in a significant way. She is the second Eve, the mother of redeemed humanity. Through her, the Word of God enters our world and overcomes death. Through her, evil loses its grasp over us, and the Word of God is born in our hearts anew. She accepted the Lord's will for her life willingly and without complaint. She looks upon each of us with a mother's heart and helps us do the same.

"Behold, your son." After he addresses his mother as "Woman," Jesus entrusts her to the disciple he loves. The beloved disciple of John's Gospel has traditionally been identified with the apostle John, the son of Zebedee.

Some exegetes, noting the complex history of the fourth Gospel, see in the figure of the beloved disciple the cumulative wisdom of the entire Johannine tradition. Because he is never specifically named in the Gospel, it has been further suggested that he represents a kind of literary type for the true believer. All disciples are truly beloved by the Lord.

In the kingdom of God, there exist no special places of honor: "...whoever wishes to be first among you shall be your slave" (Matthew 20:27).

When Jesus says to his mother, "Woman, behold, your son," he entrusts Mary not only to the beloved disciple but also to every believer. Jesus is the only begotten Son of God, and Mary is his mother. When he tells his mother to treat the beloved disciple as her son, he is explicitly recognizing the forging of new bonds and ways of relating in God's kingdom. Mary can consider the beloved disciple her son, because through his passion and death, Jesus has enabled the beloved disciple and all who believe to be called adopted sons and daughters of God.

Saint Paul makes this clear in his letter to the Romans: "For those who are led by the spirit of God are children of God. For you did not receive a spirit of slavery to fall back into fear, but you received a spirit of adoption, through which we cry, 'Abba, Father!' The Spirit itself bears witness with our spirit that we are children of God, and if children, then heirs, heirs of God and joint heirs with Christ, if only we suffer with him so that we may also be glorified with him" (Romans 8:14–17). Through his words to his mother, Jesus is declaring the basis of the new bonds being forged by his life, death, and resurrection.

Earlier in John's Gospel, Jesus tells his disciples that he no longer speaks to them as slaves, but as friends (see John 15:15). Now, as he looks down from his cross, he goes one step further. Through the words he speaks to his mother, he is telling us that he is speaking to us not only as friends, but also as brothers and sisters. These new relations are not based on blood, but on Christ's gift of the Spirit who yearns within us, "for we do not know how to pray as we ought, but the Spirit itself intercedes with inexpressible groanings" (Romans 8:26).

The beloved disciple's suffering at the foot of the cross needs also to be taken into account. We are used to thinking about Mary's participation in the sufferings of Christ's passion—as well we should. She has a unique role in the history of salvation and rightly deserves such titles of Advocate, Helper, Benefactress, and Mediatrix.

At the same time, we must not forget that others were there with her and that they also shared (albeit to a lesser degree) in the sufferings of their Lord and master. The presence of the beloved disciple at the foot of Jesus' cross reminds us that, in following Jesus, the true believer must shoulder the cross and walk a lonely path that ultimately leads to Calvary. Like the beloved disciple, they, too, stand at the foot of the cross and witness the sufferings of Christ firsthand. When we realize that Jesus is suffering in our place and that we should be the ones hanging from the wood of the cross, our love for Jesus and solidarity with him become all the more apparent.

In just a few words, Jesus has shown how the coming of the kingdom changes the way we relate to one another. His kingdom is not of this world, but it is beginning to become visible in it. Who are his mother, his brothers, and his sisters? As we have already seen, those who hear God's word and carry it out it are brother, sister, and mother to him (see Luke 8:19–21; Matthew 12:46–50; Mark 3:33–35). On one level, knowing God's will is very simple. Jesus himself says, "I give you a new commandment: love one another. As I have loved you, so you also should love one another" (John 13:34). On another level, however, knowing God's will for us means going through a process of discernment in order to understand what the most loving course of action to take might be in a particular situation. Knowing how we should love another, moreover, does not necessarily mean we have the courage and strength to carry it out. Left to our own resources, we cannot love as Jesus loved. We need help from Christ. The help he gives us comes from his spirit, who he has sent to dwell in our hearts. Mary was God's highly favored daughter (Luke 1:28), someone who was full of grace throughout her life and hence full of the spirit.

As Jesus dies on the cross, he looks down at his mother and upon all true believers. As he commends his spirit to the Father, he knows that the spirit will guide those he has left behind and that his mother will be there for his fellow brothers and sisters in their time of need.

"Behold, your mother." When Jesus finishes speaking with his mother, he turns to the beloved disciple and entrusts him to his mother. Through these words, Jesus makes Mary the mother of every true believer. Mary, who conceived by the Holy Spirit (Luke 1:35) and who was at the heart of the small company of believers at Pentecost (Acts 1:14), is traditionally considered the mother of the Church. To be the mother of the Church means she gave birth to the Church.

What does it mean to give birth to the Church? The Church,

we are told, is the Body of Christ and all who believe are members of it through faith (1 Corinthians 12:27). Mary conceived and gave birth to Christ by the power of the Spirit. Her humble fiat made this possible.

It also gives birth to the faith of his body, the Church. Meister Eckhart, the fourteenth-century Dominican theologian and mystic, speaks about the three births of the Word of God. The first birth is the Word who is eternally generated from the Father. The second birth is the Word who was born of the virgin mother at the Incarnation. The third birth is the Word who is born in our hearts through faith. We can think of Mary as the mother of the Church in this last sense. Her words to the Angel Gabriel provide us with all the evidence we need: "I am the handmaid of the Lord. May it be done to me according to your word" (Luke 1:38). When she gave her fiat to God, Mary became the first to believe in the Good News of all that God would accomplish in her son. She would not have given physical birth to Word of God had she not first given birth to him spiritually in her heart. From her simple, trusting faith, the faith of the Church was born.

Since Mary was the first to believe in Jesus, the faith of all other believers comes through her. Filled with the Spirit and interceding for us on our behalf, she gives birth to the Word of God within our hearts. When Jesus gives Mary to John as his mother, he merely recognizes a bond that has already existed. From the first moment the beloved disciple believed in Jesus, Mary became his mother. The same is true for us.

From the moment Jesus entrusted his mother to him, the beloved disciple took her into his care. As parents grow old, they are often cared for by their children. Jesus would never have the opportunity to care for his aging mother.

The beloved disciple, we are told, took that task upon himself. He took her not only into his home, but also into his heart. He loved her as his own mother, making sure that her needs were met and that she was treated with respect.

We can envision the beloved disciple sharing his troubles and concerns with Mary and going over the events of the day. We can imagine them eating together, enjoying each other's company, and celebrating in silence that special bond between a loving mother and her child. We can see Mary listening to all that the beloved disciple has to say and pondering it in her heart, in much the same way that she did with all that had been said of Jesus (see Luke 2:19).

By taking Jesus' mother into his care, the beloved disciple received her unconditional love and support in return. In a very real way, *he* was also taken into *her* care. He would never be far from her prayerful gaze.

We, too, are called to take Mary, Jesus' mother, into our care. To do so, we must bring her into our homes and also into our hearts. We bring Mary into our homes by placing small reminders of her in our midst (icons, statues, pictures, etc.).

We bring her into our hearts by praying to her and bringing to her our every need. Because Mary is the mother of God and of the Church, every Catholic Church has a shrine in or close to the sanctuary in honor of Mary.

Since the parish church is the spiritual home of the local believing community, the presence of this shrine makes a powerful statement about Mary's importance to believers. The Eastern Christian has a strong tradition of placing a holy icon, often one of the madonna and child, near the entrance of a home that is to be venerated upon entering in order to remind a person of God and the call to sanctity. Roman Catholics do something similar by placing small statues and paintings of Mary in their homes to remind them of their bond with her.

It makes little sense, however, to invite Mary, our mother, into our homes without also inviting her into our hearts. We are called to share our lives with Mary, not merely give shelter to her memory.

Because she was the first disciple, Mary can be considered not only our mother, but also our close, intimate friend. As we have seen in an earlier reflection, along with benevolence and reciprocity, one of the important marks of friendship is that of mutual indwelling.

We take Mary into our care by befriending her and allowing her to befriend us. We become her friend by allowing her in her unobtrusive and quiet way to spend time with us. As with all loving mothers, she wants us to talk to her and to bring her our needs. With Jesus, she carries us in her heart and longs to dwell in ours. As we have taken her into our care, she promises to do the same for us.

Conclusion

"Woman, behold your son...Behold, your mother."

Looking down from the cross, suspended between two worlds, and nearing the threshold of death, Jesus looks upon his mother and his beloved disciple and entrusts them to each other's care. His words to them show the kingdom for which he lived and died taking root in the world.

Because of his actions, human relationships have new possibilities. Our closest bonds are no longer those of blood, but those formed in faith and in the loving desire to do God's will. The spirit forges these new family bonds, and Jesus' commandment of love becomes the primary means by which they are shared.

Earlier in John's Gospel, Jesus tells his disciples that there is no greater love than to lay down one's life for one's friend (John 15:13). Jesus' death on the cross gives depth and substance to these words.

In death, as in life, he speaks a message of love to all who are willing to listen. Mary, his mother, and the beloved disciple follow him to the very end and listen intently to what he is telling them. Through his words, they come to discover what they somehow already knew deep down inside.

Jesus' death not only brings new meaning to life, but also changes the way we relate to one another. His beloved disciples understand the beauty, the power, and the cost of his message of love. They see in the two figures standing at the foot of Jesus' cross a reflection of themselves and of the bonds they, too, wish to forge for the sake of the kingdom.

The bond between Mary and the beloved disciple reminds us that the redemption of the world has a great deal to do with changing the way we think and act toward each other. As the mother of

Christ's body, the Church, Mary reminds us of the loving nature of the bonds we are called to share. Because of Jesus, we are all called to be brothers and sisters in faith. In Mary, his mother, he provides us, and all members of his family, with a deeply compassionate and caring mother.

Reflection Questions

1. If you had been alive at the time, where would you have been on the day Jesus died? Would you have betrayed him? Would you have denied him? Would you have run away? Would you have watched him die from a distance? Would you have watched him from the foot of the cross? Can you identify with one or many of these reactions to Jesus' suffering and death? Which is the most dominant?

2. What is your attitude toward Mary, Jesus' mother? Do you consider her the mother of God? Do you think she had a special role to play in the mystery of humanity's redemption? Do you think of her as your spiritual mother? Does she have a special role to play in your redemption? Do you bring your troubles and cares to her? Do you pray to her? Do you turn to her in times of need?

3. What is your attitude toward the beloved disciple? Why did he have a special place in Jesus' heart? What was it that set him apart from the other disciples? Can you see yourself in this role? Can you see yourself at the foot of the cross on the day Jesus died? Can you see yourself accepting Mary into your life and treating her as your mother?

4. Does the teaching of the three births of the Eternal Word make sense to you? Do you believe it? Do you believe that the Word of God desires to be born within your heart? Has that process already begun in you? If so, what more needs to be done? If not, what will it take to get it going? Can Mary or the beloved disciple help in any way? Can Jesus?

5. What does it mean to receive Mary into your home? Have you done so? If so, how have your done it? If not, why not? What does it mean to receive Mary into your heart? Have you done so? If so, how? If not, what is keeping you from doing so? Does receiving Mary into your heart have anything to do with the birth of the Word within your heart? Could there be a possible connection?

Prayer

Lord, I picture myself at the foot of your cross, beside Mary, your mother, and the beloved disciple. I can just as easily see myself, however, hiding in fear after having denied you like Peter or, worse yet, after having betrayed you like Judas. I want to follow you, Lord, but find myself weak and easily swayed. Help me, Lord, help me. Help me to be a faithful disciple. Help me to follow you all the way, through thick and through thin, in each and every circumstance. Help me also to turn to Mary in my time of need. Help me to seek her prayer and intercession and to receive her as my mother both in my home and in my heart. Help me, like her, to proclaim your greatness and your mighty deeds. Mary, my mother, pray and intercede for me. Help me to remain faithful to your Son to the very end.

Chapter Four

Abandoned by God

"My God, my God, why have you forsaken me?"

MATTHEW 27:46

As he neared death, Jesus looked down from his cross and consoled his mother and beloved disciple. They could not comfort him, however, for he was about to go someplace where they could not follow. The path before him was lonely and desolate; he had to face it by himself, with no companions. Alone in his suffering, Jesus turned to his heavenly Father and experienced him in a way he never had before. He, too, was remote and silent. In taking humanity's sins upon himself, Jesus was made to feel the full pain of complete separation from God. In his hour of need, Jesus had nothing to fall back on but his own human frailty. From his deep inner torment, he felt a keen sense of abandonment. No one would take this cup of suffering from him. He had to drink it all by himself—every last drop.

As his suffering mounted and as his moment of death drew near, Jesus found the strength to give voice to his inner anguish and cried out in a loud voice, "'*Eli, Eli, lema sabachthani?,*' that is, 'My God, my God, why have you forsaken me?'" (Matthew 27:46). These words convey a deep sense of Jesus' complete and utter isolation. In his final moments, he would lose the sense of the Father's presence to him, something he had felt continually throughout his life and that had formed the basis of his entire life and mission. Alone in his torments, Jesus now could do nothing but despair of or trust in the Father's love. His cry of anguish expresses trust, for it alludes to a psalm about the passion and ultimate triumph of the Messiah. Jesus may not have had the strength to pray all of Psalm 22. The few words that he did manage to utter, however, point to where he heart was. Once again, the words Jesus uttered invite close scrutiny.

"My God, my God." Jesus' first words come as something as a surprise. In all of the Gospel accounts and, as one must assume, throughout most of his life, he addresses God as "Abba, Father." Now, in his moment of dire need, he reverts to a more formal means of address. Why does he not cry out "My Father, my Father" instead? Would not these the words have sprung more spontaneously from his lips? Did he not teach his own disciples to pray in this way and to bring to the Father their every need? Why does he refrain from talking to God in more intimate terms? The answers to these questions lie deep within the suffering heart of Jesus and will never be fully known to us. Because we have not entered into the depths of his suffering, we can only ponder the possible meanings of his unexpected choice of words.

There is, for example, a parallel with the way Jesus addresses his mother, Mary, in the Gospel of John. By referring to Mary as a woman rather than as his mother (see John 19:26), he highlights her universal significance for humanity in his redemptive suffering. In a similar way, in Matthew's Gospel, he cries out "My God, my God" *("Eli, Eli")* as a way of emphasizing the universal dimensions of his death on the cross. Jesus cries out to God on behalf of all humanity. In doing so, he addresses God not in the intimate way to which he had grown accustomed, but in a more formal tone befitting humanity's sinful condition. Through his redemptive suffering, Jesus comes face to face with divine justice. By addressing God in this formal manner, he brings into focus the divine drama between justice and mercy that is taking place within his heart and causing him so much pain.

Another reason for Jesus to cry out, "My God, my God," may be to emphasize his solidarity with humanity. The Father reveals himself to humanity through his Son. Jesus is both God and man. He enjoys such close intimacy with the divine that he calls God, "Abba, Father." Jesus comes to this understanding by way of his divine nature. Only the Son of God could enjoy such intimacy with God. It was through his divine nature that he reveals this understanding of God to his disciples.

On the cross, however, Jesus wishes to identify himself very closely with our broken humanity. He wants to be like us in all things but sin (see Hebrews 4:15). He takes it upon himself to address God on our behalf, using the words of address with which we were most familiar. He addresses God not as "Abba, Father," which he used by virtue of his divinity, but as *"Eli, Eli"* (My God, my God), which he knew by virtue of his sharing in our common humanity. Jesus' cry from the cross to God is the cry of all humanity. He cries out in a loud voice so that all could hear him. This cry swells from deep within his heart and from deep within ours.

It is the cry that each of us utters as we face our dying moments. It is a familiar cry, a human cry, one that we have heard before. Because it comes from innocent lips, it is also a cry that is also able to penetrate the mystery of the divine. Jesus' cry from the cross echoes down the corridors of time. It is a cry of abandonment and desperation, a cry of the anguish of our human situation.

Yet another reason for Jesus' words may come from his deep experience of abandonment by God. He died on the cross so that sin and death would no longer have a hold over us. For this to happen, however, he had to take our place and suffer the consequences of sin. As Saint Paul tells us, "the wages of sin is death" (Romans 6:23). Jesus suffered and died to pay those wages on our behalf: "Just as in Adam all die, so too in Christ shall all be brought to life" (1 Corinthians 15:22). Saint Paul describes Jesus as the new Adam who brings life to the world by taking humanity's sin upon his shoulders. In this role, Jesus undergoes all the suffering required of humanity by the divine justice.

The greatest effect of Adam's sin, however, is not death itself, but the experience of being cut off from and abandoned by God. Sin disrupts our relationship with the divine. Adam's sin, what we call today the sin of human origins, did so in a very drastic and fundamental way. Jesus' cry from the cross gives external expression to his intense inner suffering resulting from his feeling of being abandoned by God. His cry is not one of despair (he *does* indeed call out to God), but of intense loneliness and inner desolation. This feeling of abandonment by God represents the climax of his passion.

Up until now, Jesus always had the intimate love of his Father to fall back on. Now, his suffering is not merely physical, psychological, and social, but also spiritual. So intense is his feeling of abandonment by the Father that Jesus cannot even bring himself to utter the name he had grown used to calling him, that is, "Abba, Father." The cross was an intense desert experience for Jesus. If he was tempted while hanging from it, one has to wonder if it had something to do with his understanding of the Father's love for him. What father would allow such a thing to happen to his loving son? How could he allow him to suffer such a horrible death? Why would he not permit this cup of suffering to pass?

Yet another reason for Jesus' choice of words comes from the very nature of God himself. No human expression can completely exhaust the mystery of the divine. The names we give to God necessarily fall short of his infinite majesty. The Jews of Jesus' day had a very strong sense of God's transcendent nature, and it was for this very reason that they thought it blasphemy if they allowed his name to pass through their lips. Jesus reacted against this Jewish custom by teaching his disciples to address God on the most intimate of human terms. God was "Abba," their Father in heaven who looked out for their every need: "Are not two sparrows sold for a small coin? Yet not one of them falls to the ground without your Father's knowledge. Even all the hairs of your head are counted. So do not be afraid; you are worth more than many sparrows" (Matthew 10:29–31).

When used as an expression for God, even the term, "Father," however, has some inherent limitations. To speak of God as "Father" makes little sense without the complementary designation of God as "Mother." The two concepts depend on each other and cannot be separated without doing serious damage to them. One reason why Jesus cries out, "My God, my God" *("Eli, Eli")* may be to remind us of this elusive quality of the divine mystery. God is "Abba, Father," to Jesus, but also so very much more. The names we can attribute to the divine are infinite; they cannot be numbered. God is Father, Mother, Brother, Sister, Lover, Friend, and so much more to us. He is also the negation of each of these terms. The divine mystery lies so much beyond our feeble attempts to understand it that some insist that the best way of describing who God is is to say what he is not. When seen in this light, God is "Father" and "not Father," "Son and "not Son," "Spirit" and "not Spirit." Jesus' repetition of the phrase "My God" may represent more than a lonely act of quiet desperation. Perhaps it is Jesus' attempt to point out the limitations of human words when they come face to face with the mystery of the divine.

"Why have you forsaken me?" Jesus' next words formulate a question. Jesus can accept the physical and mental torment of the cross. His abandonment by the Father, however, is almost too much to bear. He does not understand why, in his hour of need, the one he relied upon the most to get him through should leave him to himself. Was it not bad enough that many of his closest followers would desert him? Why must God abandon him as well? Jesus, the Word of God, does not understand the terrible ways of this mysterious divine wisdom. He questions God about the reason for this his spiritual isolation. With the Father, he could accept the obedience of the cross and suffer his fate quietly and without lament. Without the Father, however, he feels overpowered by the gathering shadows of death that encompass him.

What makes matters even worse is that he receives no response. The Father's abandonment of his Son at the moment of his death is complete and total. Jesus receives no consolation whatsoever. God has abandoned him to humanity's fate. Jesus suffers in our place and has felt the full weight of humanity's separation from God. This deep spiritual isolation from the Father was Jesus' descent into hell, that is, the state of eternal separation from God.

Jesus entered that state on our behalf. By bonding his humanity to us, he accepted our fate as his own. Because he was God, what would have been an eternity for us lasted but a single moment: "With the Lord one day is like a thousand years and a thousand years like one day" (2 Peter 3:8).

The Father, however, has not done this to Jesus. We are the ones who have caused it. Jesus was left utterly alone to face his approaching death. In that aloneness, he carried the weight of humanity's sins. Our sins, our deeply ingrained egoism and self-centeredness, have brought about Jesus' isolation. The Father abandoned him because we abandoned the Father. God has forsaken him because we, by our own choice, have chosen to forsake the divine.

Jesus' abandonment by God embraced every dimension of his being: the physical, the emotional, the mental, the social, and especially the spiritual. In this tortured state, he entered the depths of our broken humanity and brought it back to wholeness. He did so by confronting the powers of darkness with the power of love.

His death on the cross would ultimately show that love was stronger than death and formed the underlying fabric of reality. As he hung from the cross, however, all this remained mysteriously hidden from sight. Abandoned by his Father at this critical juncture of his life, he had one fundamental choice before him: to despair of life and of all he hoped for or to trust that, even though it seemed so distant and far away, the love of the Father would ultimately be there for him. Jesus chose the latter and never doubted his decision.

As noted earlier, these words of Jesus echo the opening of Psalm 22. By saying these words, Jesus was invoking the entire psalm. He uttered them first to express his deep sense of abandonment and isolation from God. The appropriateness of the psalm is astounding, for it even recounts Jesus' manner of execution: "So wasted are my hands and feet that I can count all my bones. They stare at me and gloat; they divide my garments among them; for my clothing they cast lots" (Psalm 22:17–19). By uttering these words, Jesus associates all of his passion and death with the sentiments of the psalmist. These feelings are much more complex than the desperate cry of abandonment that the psalm's opening words suggest. When read in its entirety, the psalm actually represents an eloquent prayer of hope and trust in the power of God to save.

Jesus singles this psalm out from all the others for a reason. As we read the psalm, it gradually turns from a cry of desperation to one of thanksgiving, trust, even praise. By uttering its opening words, Jesus wished to display his deep trust in the Father, regardless of what he was feeling at the time. The change in tone is astonishing. From a cry of desolation it turns into a plea for help: "Do not stay far from me, for trouble is near, and there is no one to help" (Psalm 22:12). From this cry for help, the psalmist calls upon the Lord with more and more assurance: "Deliver me from the sword, my forlorn life from the teeth of the dog" (Psalm 22:21). His words gradually reveal his utmost trust and confidence in what the power of God can accomplish: "Save me from the lion's mouth, my poor life from the horns of wild bulls" (Psalm 22:22). From there, the psalmist breaks out into a song of praise: "Then I will proclaim your name to the assembly; in the community I will praise you: 'You who fear the LORD, give praise! All descendants of Jacob, give honor; show reverence, all descendants of Israel!'" (Psalm 22:23–24).

Regardless of what has happened, Jesus wishes to demonstrate his complete and utter trust in the Father's plan for him. In accordance with the Father's will, he has obediently accepted death. He has turned to the Lord in his time of need and trusts that he (and the humanity he represents) will not be forgotten. The psalm's final verse makes Jesus' hope abundantly clear: "The generation to come will be told of the LORD, that they may proclaim to a people yet unborn the deliverance you have brought" (Psalm 22:32). Jesus' hope becomes our hope. His death on the cross demonstrates the justice of the Father in the form of the unconditional love of the Son. Since the Father and the Son are one (see John 10:30), so are God's justice and love. Jesus represents both the love and the justice of the Father—and vice versa. On the cross of Christ, the justice and love of God penetrate each other and manifest themselves to us in the form of divine mercy. Jesus looks at us from his cross and asks us to go and do likewise.

As he hung from the cross, the question Jesus puts to God remains unanswered. During this time of suffering, Jesus could search for his Father's presence only in the quiet solitude of his heart. Jesus had to suffer the fate of humanity before the Father's response could become evident. Only by dying could the Son of Man be raised. Only by descending into hell could he ascend to his rightful place at the Father's right hand.

Despite the silence of the Father, Jesus, in his hour of need, chooses trust over despair. That choice was taken on our behalf and has become for us a legacy of hope. Because of it, we can picture ourselves in his place when we look to the cross. *"Eli, Eli, lema sabachthani?"* become our words; Psalm 22, our prayer; the cross, a sign for us of God's unbroken trust. Jesus suffered the horrors of the cross in order to pass beyond them. The Father raised him on the third day. The day will come when he will do the same for us.

Conclusion

"My God, my God, why have you forsaken me?"

Uttering these words from the cross, Jesus reveals himself to us as a deep man of prayer. His words of lamentation come from a heart already broken by human ingratitude and soon to be pierced by a soldier's lance. That heart opens in a cry of desperation, looking for some consolation from a God who now seems strangely absent. Jesus cries out to God and questions him. "Why have you forsaken me?" It is a question we all ask at some point in our sojourn through life. It is a question about suffering and death. It is a question about the meaning of life and ultimately about our need for God.

God's response to Jesus' prayer comes in the mounting silence. Jesus, the Word of God, yearns for a word of consolation and comes face-to-face with a mysterious void. Jesus must face his suffering by himself. He must die alone, with nothing but our sins and human frailty to attend him. God is absent because we have made it so. He cannot commune with hearts that have voluntarily turned away from him. Jesus has never done so, but he has taken our place. We have done so many times—too many to be numbered.

The moment comes, however, when the day of salvation finally arrives. The silence of God swells up inside Jesus' darkened sepulcher. It fills his lifeless corpse and breathes new life into it. The silence of the Father speaks. It communes with the Word in the beating motion of Jesus' heart.

"My God, my God!" The Father responds to Jesus' cry. He rolls back the stone of death and raises his Son from the grave. Jesus opens his eyes; he breathes; he swallows; he moves his lips; he speaks.

He finds himself alive—back from the dead—existing in a transformed state. The silence of God has defeated death. It communes in Jesus' heart. The Father speaks and is reunited with his Son. The two are as one; they instill within our hearts a deep longing to believe.

Jesus continues to dwell in our midst. His kingdom lives on. The will of the Father has been accomplished.

Reflection Questions

1. Have you ever felt isolated and alone by others? By God? If so, how did you cope with the situation? Did it last for a long time? Did it increase or diminish over time? Did you learn anything from the experience? Did you find it difficult to talk with others? Did you find it difficult to talk with God?

2. What dimensions of human suffering have visited you most frequently? The physical? The emotional? The mental? The social? The spiritual? Which do you find most difficult to deal with? Is there any combination of these that you have found particularly traumatic? How have you coped with it?

3. Do you find it easy or difficult to trust God? Is it easier for you to trust him in some circumstances more than others? If so, which kinds of situations make it easy to trust him? In which situations do you find it more difficult to trust him? Have you ever felt abandoned by God? If so, were you able to trust him in that situation? Were you able to pray to him?

4. Are you able to question God? Can you ask him why things have happened and turned out the way they did? If not, what is keeping you from doing so? Does God invite such questions or discourage them? What can be gained from asking such questions? Why did Jesus ask such questions from the cross? Does such questioning draw one closer to God or further apart?

5. Why do you think Jesus used the psalms to call on God in his hour of need? Do you think he did so often? Was he able to pray them from the heart? How else could he have prayed them? Do you use the psalms in prayer? If so, is there any one in particular that you find particularly helpful? If not, would you be willing to try reflecting upon them? Do you think you can pray them from the heart?

Prayer

~~~~~~~~~~~~~~

Lord, I see you hanging from the cross in the midst of your abandonment and crying out to God. You ask him a simple question and receive only silence for a response. I, too, find myself hanging from a cross, Lord. I too cry out to God. I, too, ask why. All too often, I feel as though I am not given any answers. At those times, I am tempted to lose faith and give up hope. Lord, help me to never give in to such temptations. Help me to turn to you, especially during times of loneliness and when I am feeling abandoned. Help me to make peace with the silence that envelops me in my pain. Help me to cry out to God with all my heart. Lord, help me to discover the word God is speaking to me within the silence and in my experience of abandonment. Help me to listen and believe ever more firmly that I am being listened to in my time of need. Mary, my mother, pray for me.

Chapter Five

Thirsting for God

"I thirst."

JOHN 19:28

With death approaching, Jesus' body shows signs of wear. He has not eaten or drunk since he celebrated his last meal with his closest disciples the night before. Since then, the hours have passed slowly, and he has not been given the chance to rest his eyes. Sleep eludes him even as his muscles ache from heavy bruises, and fatigue invades his weary bones. His mouth is parched and dry. He longs to wet his lips. He can barely swallow. "I thirst," he says, in a barely audible whisper.

It is a wonder that any of the soldiers beneath the cross can hear him. Nearby there is a jar of sour wine spiked with myrrh. One of the soldiers soaks a sponge in this wine, places it on a stick of hyssop, raises it to Jesus' lips and tries to make him drink

(John 19:29–30). This sip of wine heralds Jesus' entrance into his kingdom. Those beneath him watch him bow his head and lower his breathing. His final moments are upon him. Those watching him are amazed at the lack of complaint with which he faces his impending death. All eyes are upon him, even those of his executioners.

Jesus' thirst from the cross draws those around him closer. We listen to his words, but can barely hear him. He touches us, because we recognize the humanness of his plight. Jesus' thirst puts us in touch with our own. We see him hanging from the cross and imagine ourselves in his place. Our thirst is not all that different from his.

We, too, are bloodied, weary, and aching. We, too, are in dire need of rest. We, too, are about to die. Jesus' parched lips remind us of our own that yearn to be sponged and wetted. His words heighten our memories and force us to confront our deep, inner yearnings.

"I thirst." These words could easily be those of a child. Thirst is such a basic human need, and children want their appetites to be satisfied. It has been said that, as we approach death, we tend to revert to the ways of our early childhood.

As Jesus nears death, he, too, looks out on the world as a small, helpless child. He once told his disciples: "Amen, I say to you, unless you turn and become like children, you will not enter the kingdom of heaven" (Matthew 18:3). As he faces death and is about to step beyond its shadowy pale, he becomes increasingly childlike in his bearing. It is only because of him, the Son of God, that we are able to call ourselves "children of God." It is through Jesus that we become the Father's adopted sons and daughters.

Death makes helpless children of us all. We can do nothing to fight or ward it off. Sooner or later, it finds us and exacts its devastating toll. We hunger and thirst for life but ultimately must take a draught from its dark, murky well. We know not when it comes. When we sense its approach, we shirk away from it in fear. No one can hide from it. We try to deny its hold over us, but soon feel its cold, bony hands tightening around us.

We try to bargain with it, hoping to convince it to leave us alone, if only just for a while. But bargaining holds little sway with death, for it holds all the cards. Even in the face of our anger and outrage, it simply looks back at us with its cold, silent stare. It haunts us in our sleep, refusing to let us rest. It stalks us quietly wherever we go, staking its claim on us and on those we love.

Our only respite is to accept death by relinquishing our claim to life and allowing it to take from us that which we hold most precious. Jesus faced death in this way. He experienced every human fear, trauma, hunger, and thirst. He found himself helpless before death, like an innocent child. His thirst was more than physical: it was a thirst for life, a craving that his impending death could not quench.

Hanging from the cross, Jesus cries out with the psalmist: "As dry as a potsherd is my throat; my tongue sticks to my palate; you lay me in the dust of death" (Psalm 22:16). Like all of us, Jesus faces the dust of death. He, too, is dust and must one day return to dust (see Genesis 3:19). Only the Father's love can brush aside this dismal and dreary fate.

There are many kinds of thirst, and Jesus experienced them all. The most obvious of them is the physical. As he hung from the cross, Jesus craved for water with which he could wet his mouth and cleanse the sweat and dirt from his blood-caked skin.

Ever since his arrest the evening before, he had been put through a terrible physical ordeal. He had been scourged, mocked, spat upon, crowned with thorns, and made to carry his own cross outside the city gates to his place of execution. All that had led up to his crucifixion was probably enough to kill him. He was now nailed to the cross and left to hang until every ounce of his strength was sapped and he could barely breathe. Death would come to him by way of asphyxiation. As his final moments approached, one can well imagine how much he would have appreciated a small sip of cool, refreshing water to ease his pain.

Water had always been a powerful symbol for Jesus. He began his public ministry by being baptized in the Jordan (Mark 1:9–11). He used it to perform his first public miracle, changing water into wine at Cana (John 2:1–12). At Sychar, he asked a Samaritan woman to draw some water from Jacob's well so that he could quench his thirst in the heat of the sun (John 4:4–7). In conversation with this woman, he had even promised to be the bearer of "living water" that would quench every thirst and bring eternal life to all who drank it (John 4:10–14). After his death, water mixed with blood would be seen flowing from his side (John 19:34).

Wherever Jesus was, water never seemed to be very far away. During his execution, however, there was no water for him to wet his lips and soothe his dried-out tongue and palate. The lack of it enhanced his suffering, making his death all the more terrible.

Jesus also thirsted for consolation. His experience of the past twenty-four hours had completely drained his emotional strength. After his Last Supper with his closest disciples, his world began to unravel. Judas had betrayed him. Peter had denied him. With the exception of a few women and the beloved disciple, all the rest of his followers had fled out of fear of what might happen to them.

Jesus had been abandoned by everyone, even by his Father in heaven. Humanly speaking, Jesus had been put through a period of keen emotional strain. The psychological toll was enormous. As he hung from his cross, he must have mourned the loss of these treasured relationships. Nothing could be said. Nothing could be done to get them back. Everything he had lived for was gone. His closest friends had disowned him. His mission to God's people lay in ruins. Everything had been taken away from him, even his clothing.

The words of Job describe his fate: "Naked I came forth from my mother's womb, and naked shall I go back again" (Job 1:21). Hanging virtually naked from his cross, Jesus suffered numerous psychological torments. He died a broken man. As death approached, even his most basic of emotional needs were left unmet.

Jesus also thirsted for the kingdom. He believed that his suffering and death on the cross was somehow connected with its coming. His kingdom, as he had told Pontius Pilate, was not of this world (see John 18:36). It belonged not to this world, but to the world of his Father in heaven. "Your kingdom come, your will be done on earth as in heaven" (Matthew 6:10), he had taught his disciples to pray. For him, the coming of the kingdom was closely connected with doing the will of the Father.

He was convinced that doing the will of God would make the kingdom present on the earth. He believed that his suffering and death was in accordance with the will of the Father. By accepting it without complaint, he believed the kingdom manifested itself on earth. Jesus lived and died to do the will of his Father. He lived and died for the kingdom. He embodied the kingdom and made it present to us through his life, as well as through his death. He did not fully understand the reason for his suffering and death. He only knew that it was the Father's will for him.

"I am the way and the truth and the life" (John 14:6), he told his disciples. That way, for him, was closely tied to the way of the cross. The path of Jesus was intimately tied to his person. He asks us to follow him into his kingdom by taking up our crosses and following in his footsteps (see Matthew 16:24). That choice is ours for the making. Like Jesus, we, too, thirst for the kingdom. We, too, make it present by doing the Father's will. By his life and death, Jesus reveals to us the true meaning of the Father's will for us: "I give you a new commandment: love one another. As I have loved you, so you also should love one another" (John 13:34). He asks us to take these words to heart.

We cannot understand Jesus' thirst for the kingdom, however, unless we recognize his deep love for humanity. Jesus thirsted not only for the kingdom of the Father, but also for the whole human family. He loved us with all of his heart, mind, soul, and strength. He longed to share with us the deep intimacy that he shared with the Father.

That intimacy with the Father we have come to recognize as his spirit. His gift of the spirit to us allows us to thirst for things he thirsted for. What he yearned most for was to dwell within our hearts. He could do so only by sharing his spirit with us: "Amen, amen, I say to you, no one can enter the kingdom of God without being born of water and Spirit." (John 3:5). Jesus' words to Nicodemus remind us of the close connection between the coming of the kingdom and the gift of the spirit. "What is born of flesh is flesh and what is born of spirit is spirit" (John 3:6).

Pentecost could not have happened without Jesus' resurrection. His resurrection could not have happened without his passion and death. Jesus thirsted on the cross for the coming of the spirit into the human heart. Through Jesus' suffering and death, humanity was begotten from above. The spirit was released by the dying breath of God's only begotten Son. Because of the Son's love for us, the spirit was free to roam the earth and blow wherever it pleased (see John 3:8).

Jesus' thirst from the cross gives us a new understanding of the nature of God's love. Spiritual writers often speak about two important dimensions of love: *love as gift* and *love as need*. When most of us think of love, we easily identify it with the notion of giving. Jesus, we say, entered our world, gave himself to us completely, to the point of dying for us, in order to become food and nourishment for us, and our source of hope. It is easy for us to associate gift-love with divine love. God loves us by giving himself to us. Our very existence is possible because he sustains us in being from one moment to the next.

It is much more difficult, however, for us to think of God's love in terms of a divine need. Part of the reason for this difficulty is the traditional image we have of God as being the epitome of perfection. God for us is omniscient, omnipotent, and unchanging. Because he is eternal, God has no contingencies. He always was, is, and will be the same. Such a God, we believe, can never be in need. To need someone or some thing is a sign of limitation and weakness.

God, we somehow convince ourselves, cannot need anything because he is infinite and limitless. We find it easy to speak about our need for God, but have much more difficulty thinking in terms of God's need for us. Jesus' thirst on the cross helps us to relate to God in a totally different way.

Jesus represents both God's gift to humanity and humanity's gift to God. As God's gift to humanity, he is the redeemer. Through his death on the cross, Jesus made humanity's fellowship with God once again possible. God's gift to us implies a need on our part. Jesus did for us something we were unable to do for ourselves. Because of our egoism and self-centeredness, it was impossible for us to rectify our relationship with God. Human nature had somehow gone awry, and only God himself could make it right again.

Becoming man was God's way of straightening things out. By entering our world and becoming one of us, God was able to intercede for us on our behalf. Jesus continues to do so for us to this very day. He is our means to the Father, the path each of us must follow to pass from this life to life eternal.

As humanity's gift to God, Jesus represents a unique opportunity. God created the world out of love. He sustains it out of love. As creator, however, there is one thing God could not do: experience creation from within. Humanity is creation coming to a consciousness of itself. In the Incarnation, humanity provides God with the opportunity to experience his creation from the inside looking out. Humanity's gift to God is the ability to experience life through human eyes. God created us in his image and likeness not only out of love, but also out of a desire to perceive creation through creation's eyes. To see, to hear, to taste, to touch, to smell as a human being—these are the gifts that humanity gives to God. Jesus presents these gifts to the Father on our behalf. Because he and the Father are one, we have the hope of sharing in an intimate relationship with him.

Gift-love and need-love are two sides of the same coin. It is impossible to have one without the other. God does not need us in the same way we need him. His needs, however, are no less real. God's greatest need is the need to love. In the person of Jesus, that need reaches the greatest of heights: both human and divine. Our need for God and God's need for us converge in the person of Jesus. God's gift to us and our gift to God also converge in him.

Jesus' thirst from the cross reminds us that God cannot be conveniently categorized by our preconceived notions of divinity. Saint Paul reminds us that the preaching of Christ crucified was "…a stumbling block to Jews and foolishness to Gentiles" (1 Corinthians 1:23). Neither group was able to get beyond their biases concerning the nature of the Godhead. The cross of Jesus is a sign of contradiction. When we see him thirsting from it, we understand the nature of God's love in a completely different light.

Finally, Jesus' thirst from the cross puts us in touch with the many thirsts of our own human situation. Every dimension of our human makeup gives us something to yearn for and long after.

In addition to our bodily wants, we thirst for emotional support, intellectual challenges, human understanding, and spiritual wholeness. We yearn for holiness and wholeness, for health and wellness, for solitude and companionship, for peace and justice. Jesus once said to his disciples, "Blessed are they who hunger and thirst for righteousness, for they will be satisfied" (Matthew 5:6).

Our deepest thirst concerns our need for God. The closer we get to God, the more intense this thirst becomes. Our thirst for God can never be quenched. The more we drink of the life-giving water of the spirit, the more we desire to live and move and to have our being in the divine mystery.

A saint is someone whose thirst for God is in the forefront of his or her thoughts, words, and actions. He or she is conformed to the life of Christ and, in doing so, has actually become "another Christ" (*alter Christus*) for the world.

The Church is made up of a veritable communion of saints. These people perpetuate Christ's presence in the world. Through them, Christ's message and mission continues. They are sent "to bring glad tidings to the poor. He has sent me to proclaim liberty to captives and recovery of sight to the blind, to let the oppressed go free" (Luke 4:18). They are Jesus' eyes, ears, and arms in the world today.

They thirst for what Jesus most thirsted for: the in-breaking of the kingdom into the human heart. Jesus' thirst from the cross is thus a holy thirst. It yearns for the union of the human heart with the divine and of the divine heart with the human. It longs for the coming together of the two and cannot wait until they penetrate each other.

Even though he felt abandoned by the Father, Jesus felt this holy thirst intensely. Through his sacrifice on the cross, he imparts this thirst to his followers. Those who pick up their crosses and walk in his footsteps experience the same intense yearning for humanity's reconciliation with God.

Conclusion

"I thirst."

These words of Jesus from the cross contain many layers of meaning. Those who ponder them soon recognize the depth of Jesus' longing for humanity. He wanted more than just water to wet his tongue and to ease his pain. Jesus' thirst represents, at one and the same time, both God's yearning for humanity, and humanity's yearning for God. In him, the two have become inseparable.

As we draw closer to death, we come face to face with our thirsts. We look to Jesus and recognize that he has gone before us. By uniting ourselves to him, his thirst becomes our thirst; our thirst, his. He himself assures us: "Whoever drinks the water I shall give will never thirst; the water I shall give will become in him a spring of water welling up to eternal life" (John 4:14).

That life-giving water flowed from Jesus' side after his death. It welled up within the community of disciples in the upper room when they were filled with the spirit in the early-morning hours and boldly proclaimed the good news of Jesus' rising from the dead.

It flowed from the baptismal font when we were immersed into the paschal mystery of his suffering, death, and resurrection. It wells up within us and refreshes us now—and will continue to do so for all eternity.

What must we do to receive such water? With the Samaritan woman, we need only say: "Give me this water, so that I may not be thirsty" (John 4:15). Jesus and Jesus alone can give this water to us. He alone can draw it for us. He alone can lift the ladle from the bucket to our lips and help us to sip. He alone can loosen our parched mouths and dried-out tongues. He alone can help us to swallow the cool, refreshing waters of his spirit.

The spirit of God swept over the waters like a mighty wind at creation (Genesis 1:2). The spirit of God gave form to Jesus in the waters of Mary's womb (Luke 1:35). The spirit of God swept through the upper room at Pentecost like a strong driving wind (Acts 2:2). The spirit of God leads us to refreshing waters at the moment of death. That spirit, the spirit of the Father, the spirit of Jesus, the Holy Spirit, even now intercedes for us "with inexpressible groanings" (Romans 8:26). We could do nothing better than to open our hearts to him and unite our thirst to his. Jesus would have wanted it that way. It is for what he most deeply thirsted—and what we most deeply desire.

Reflection Questions

1. What was Jesus' thirst from the cross like? Was it more than physical? Did it embrace other dimensions of his existence? Was it in any way emotional? Mental? Social? Spiritual? Was he thirsting for God? Was he thirsting for the kingdom? Was he thirsting for our redemption?

2. Do you understand the difference between gift-love and need-love? Can you identify these various types of love in your own life? Do you wish to have a balance between the two? Which is predominant in you? Which do you need more of? Do you think God has both gift-love and need-love? Which do you find easier to associate with him?

3. What do you thirst for? Are there many things on your list? Or few? Where does your thirst for God fit in? Is it high up on the list? Near the bottom? Somewhere in the middle? What could you do to bring your thirst for God more to the forefront of your awareness?

4. Does your yearning and thirst for God come solely from you? What part does the Holy Spirit play in it? Have you ever experienced the spirit groaning within you? If so, who or what is it groaning for? Do you identify this groaning with spiritual thirst? If so, who or what is the spirit thirsting for? Do you think this thirst will ever go away? Should it?

5. In what sense does Jesus thirst for you? In what sense does he need you? What would it take to quench this thirst? In what sense is his thirst related to his desire to dwell within your heart? What is the living water that will quench our thirst for God? What is the living water that will quench God's thirst for us? Are the two somehow related? Are they somehow revealed to us in and through Jesus' thirst from the cross?

Prayer

~~~~~~~~~

LORD, I see you on the cross and dying not only of your wounds, but also of thirst. I know that I am at least partially to blame for what you are going through. You have experienced all human thirsts and hungers. You did so to free us from them and to replace them only with a hunger for God. Lord, I have many thirsts, many hungers, many passions and desires. I am sorry for allowing them to get out of hand and to take control of me. Help me to overcome them so that I might thirst only for God. Help me also to serve you and my brothers and sisters by seeking to quench their thirsts in their time of need. Lord, help me to give drink to the thirsty. Help me to see you in the poor and the needy. Help me to thirst for the water of life eternal, to drink it, and to share it with others. Mary, my mother, pray for me.

Chapter Six

A Courageous Death

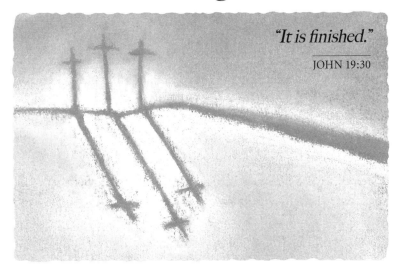

"It is finished."

JOHN 19:30

Jesus' task on earth was not complete until his life was taken from him. When he turned his face toward Jerusalem at a key point during his public ministry, he knew that he would be asked to make the ultimate sacrifice. As he hung from the cross and felt his life ebbing away from him, he sensed that the end was coming near. By offering his life, he was doing all that he could. Soon his life and mission would be out of his hands. His Father in heaven, who now seemed so very far away from him, would have to take it from there. All he could do was trust.

Earlier in John's Gospel, Jesus said that his food was to do the will of the one who had sent him (John 4:34). He also said that he would lay down his life freely and take it up again at the Father's command (John 10:18). Still later he said that finishing the work the Father had given him to do would bring glory to the Father (John 17:4). From the very beginning, Jesus knew where his mission was to take him. He came to give witness to the glory of the Father's kingdom. This was his food and nourishment. This was the Father's command.

It is hard to fathom the depth of Jesus' relationship to the Father. The bond of love between them was so strong that the Son would freely take upon his shoulders the task of humanity's redemption. His death by crucifixion was a necessary part of that mission. The sacrifice at Calvary was Jesus' most defining moment. He did not flinch when he grew weary or when the task before him became difficult. He kept his focus and carried through with it to the very end. Through his death on the cross, Jesus gave witness to his love for the Father and to his love for us. When his mission was consummated, heaven and earth were united by that love. His words remind us of the courage with which he offered himself—to the very end.

"*It is finished.*" Jesus' mission had a very specific goal: the liberation of God's people. To further this task, he led a life of teaching and healing that opened up a new dimension of God's love for the human race. Jesus represents the fullness of God's revelation. This fullness was demonstrated not only in Jesus' life, but also in his passion and death. Jesus' death on the cross demonstrates the extent of God's love for humanity. To save us from death, God was willing not only to become one of us, but also to offer his life for us. The offering of Jesus from the cross was fully human, but also fully divine. In Jesus, we cannot separate the two. What he offered in his humanity can also be said of his divinity—and vice versa.

Jesus was relieved to see his end in sight. He could sense his journey drawing to a close. To understand the magnitude of what he had accomplished, it is important for us to see his death as the culmination of an offering of self that began long before his brief sojourn on earth began. Jesus' *kenosis*, or self-emptying, stems from his very nature.

As the Word of God, he listens intently to the will of the Father and, regardless of the cost, seeks to bring it about: "Though he was in the form of God, (he) did not regard equality with God something to be grasped. Rather, he emptied himself, taking the form of a slave, coming in human likeness" (Philippians 2:6–7). The Word of God does not return in vain (see Isaiah 55:11). When it entered Mary's womb and took on human flesh, it was carrying out the will of God. Because of Mary's fiat, it was also carrying out the will of humanity.

The Incarnation united in the person of Jesus the will of both God and man. Because of that union, we are able to commune with the Father in a special way. Jesus' suffering and death on the cross sealed the bond of this new relationship. Through his passion and death, we have the opportunity to share in his spirit and be united with him and the Father in a way we never before thought possible.

When Jesus said, "It is finished," however, we should not get the idea that he was eager to stop giving himself. These words are those of a dying man and do not make any claims for what might happen beyond death. These words apply specifically to the end of Jesus' suffering, to the end of that part of his mission for which he was uniquely charged. At this point, there is nothing more Jesus can do. He set out to do the will of the Father and his hour is quickly drawing to a close. Soon he will be dead and buried. A large stone will be rolled in front of his tomb. In the silence of the grave, no words will be spoken.

Jesus' words from the cross show that an important chapter in the history of salvation is drawing to a close. Jesus' offering of self has gone on to the point of death. Nothing more is humanly possible. Any further giving would be up to the Father and what the Father himself would accomplish in Jesus. Jesus' dying hope—his only hope—was to trust in the love of the Father.

What Jesus could no longer do, the Father himself would have to accomplish. Although the Father seemed so distant and far away, Jesus still trusted that his dying would not be in vain. Jesus died giving testimony to his love for his Father. It was from this love that his love for humanity both sprang and would soon return. If his death were to lead to life, his Father in heaven would have to accomplish it in him. If Jesus' promise of new life were now to have any effect, it was the Father who would have to act. As Jesus lay lifeless in the tomb, only the Father could act in a way that would allow him to continue his mission of redemptive love.

In his dying moments on the cross, however, Jesus was not only giving himself as an offering of self to the Father. He was also giving himself to us. His passion and death stand as a model of courage for his followers to imitate. Down through the centuries, generation upon generation of Christians would look to the cross and see in the bloodied *corpus* hanging from it both a challenge and a call. The challenge would be to dare to trust in him as he trusted in the Father. The call would be to pick up their own crosses and follow in his steps. Jesus' cross is always challenging and calling us. No matter where we are, it stands as a reminder of someone who gave every ounce of his life for us in order that we might live. His challenge and his call ask us to do the same for others. Jesus' death on the cross seeks to evoke from us a similar response.

Because Jesus' passion and death is a historical event that can be verified and rooted in time, the courage with which he faced it contains within itself a number of distinct temporal dimensions. Jesus faced his passion and death with *expectant apprehension, enduring patience,* and *steadfast perseverance.* He was constant in his desire to do the will of the Father before, during, and after his crucifixion. He never flinched from the path he had chosen, and he walked it until it reached its end.

Expectant apprehension does not mean that Jesus was not able to enjoy the life he lived. The Gospels are full of stories revealing his zest for life and his pleasures in the simple joys of life. His parables arise from his keen observation of life, nature, and human relationships and represent a keen awareness of the Father's love for and closeness to the created order. Jesus fasted, but also feasted; he went off by himself to pray, but also was very much at home in the homes of others. He was focused on his relationship with the Father, but was also very much dedicated to others.

Despite his celebration of life, however, Jesus knew what lay ahead. He lived his life deeply conscious of the terrible passion and death that was to come. This knowledge had two effects on him. On the one hand, it made him celebrate the gift of life with even greater joy. On the other hand, it added an underlying sense of the tragic in all he did. As he went about his early life and public ministry, his very love for life must have filled him with a deep sense of anxiety at the thought of losing it. His agony in the Garden of Gethsemane the night before he died was the climax of a silent undertow of dread that accompanied him throughout his life.

Still, Jesus did not allow these feelings to take control of him. Even though he knew what he eventually would face, he did not let anything get in the way of his mission. Doing the will of the Father was first and foremost in his mind. All else was secondary and, in the long run, mattered very little.

Enduring patience means that Jesus was able to bear his suffering in the present moment. He did not ignore it or try to escape it. He stared his suffering straight in the eye and bore it with great strength and courage. Jesus' spirit could not be broken. No matter what was done to him, he refused to waver. He looked to neither the past nor the future. He suffered in the present moment, bearing the torments of his passion with patience. Looking to the cross, this word takes on new meaning for us.

The word "patience" is connected to the word "passion" and comes from the Latin word "*pati*," meaning "to suffer." Patience is not a glum and colorless secondary virtue, but an integral part of what it means to be brave. Although it is normally associated with our putting up with small inconveniences in the light of a greater good, it has direct relevance to the ultimate act of courage, that of martyrdom.

The martyr offers his or her life as a way of giving witness to God. Jesus was a martyr, for he gave his life as a witness to the Father's love for humanity. Before death, the martyr often undergoes unspeakable tortures in order to be enticed to recant. To bear such sufferings, he or she must be able to withstand them in the present moment.

The present moment can be perceived from at least two perspectives. Chronologically it is just a basic building block of time. Here, present moments are simply strung together to create measured units of time such as minutes, hours, days, and years.

From the perspective of *Kairos* or "sacred time," however, the present moment offers us a window to eternity, a fleeting glimpse into the intimate life of the Godhead. By suffering in the present moment, the martyr unites the present with the eternal and offers that suffering to God.

When seen in this light, Jesus is the martyr par excellence. As the Son of God, he alone could act as the sole mediator between the human and the divine. All other martyrs do so by participating in his suffering so as to share in the glory that he renders to the Father.

Steadfast perseverance refers to Jesus' capacity to endure the trial of his passion and death unto death. This quality of being and action accompanied Jesus throughout his life. It focuses not so much on suffering in the present moment (important as it may be), but on bearing with one's trials and lasting until the very end.

Perseverance, in this sense, focuses intensely on the final goal of one's suffering. It looks to the meaning behind this suffering and uses it to help one get through from one moment to the next. Jesus' persevering attitude helped him focus on this goal and live his life entirely in its light. That goal was the liberation of humanity from the throes of death and the reinstatement of the conditions for its communion with the Father. Jesus' suffering and death are intimately tied to this goal. As his end drew near, he focused on that goal with even greater intensity. With his pilgrimage on earth nearly ended, he prepared himself to cross the last boundary that separated humanity from God and God from humanity.

The drama of his death was bringing both factors—the human and the divine—into play. The reconciliation between God and man was taking place in the deepest recesses of his heart. As he came to his end, he recognized that something new was just beginning. The new covenant between God and humanity was being written in his blood. That blood was spilling from his wounds and flowing through his heart. With his dying breaths and the last beats of his heart, he took solace in knowing that he had remained faithful both to the Father and to us until the very end.

Jesus was a man of heart. To have heart is to exude passion for a cause and to evince a willingness to sacrifice for its concrete realization. Jesus demonstrated his heart by the way he faced the obstacles he encountered through life. His suffering on the cross was the greatest of these. It tapped his strength and drained his resources.

His executioners thought that by breaking him down physically, they could also shatter his determination and will. They managed to pierce his heart, but they could never break it. Try as they may, his heart was in another place and could not be touched. Jesus did not die from a broken, wounded heart, but from a love his human heart could no longer hold.

Hanging from his cross, he opened his heart to the Father and to humanity and invited both to commune with him. As he gave up his spirit, something moved within our own hearts. It would not be long before we discovered the life-giving power behind Jesus' death.

Jesus' suffering and death continues to this day in the members of his body. We who have been immersed in his paschal mystery participate in his suffering and death. We will be crucified on the crosses that we have shouldered for him and for his following. We will suffer innocently from wounds inflicted upon our bodies and souls.

The crucifix serves as a reminder of what Jesus went through for us and of what he is asking us to go through for him and for others. When we look at it, we are reminded that we, too, must face our suffering and eventual death with expectant apprehension, enduring patience, and steadfast perseverance.

Our joy and zest for life will be tinged with the knowledge of a death that is to come. Our suffering in the moment will serve as a window to eternity, opening us up to the intimate life of the Godhead. Our focus on the reason and end of life will help us to face our suffering and death with steadfast perseverance. Because of Jesus' suffering and death, our own suffering and death take on new meaning.

Through Christ, the power of God's love has been unleashed in the world. Jesus gives us the opportunity to share in that power and to be with him until our earthly end converges into his.

The cross of Christ, however, is more than a mere reminder. It does much more than merely inspire us or present itself to us as a model to be imitated. Christ's paschal mystery incorporates our lives and deaths into his. It also sows in us the seeds to new life. Through it, the narrative of Christ's passion, death, and resurrection becomes our own. It not only molds and shapes us, but actually allows us to enter into to it and become an integral part of its ongoing historical unfolding. Christ did not only suffer, die, and rise some two thousand years ago. He is doing so constantly today in the members of his body.

Our union with him through the waters of baptism allows us to continue his mission of liberation. He continues to suffer and die in us until his task is complete in this day and age. In us, he continues to strive to carry out the will of the Father. Through us, he will not relent until, seeing the end in sight, he can say yet another time: "It is finished."

Jesus suffers in us, and we suffer in him. The mystery of Christ's passion and death extends to those who follow in his footsteps and call upon his name. That mystery becomes comprehensible to us, however, only in the light of the empty tomb. The Easter proclamation gives us new eyes with which to ponder the meaning of Jesus' self-offering and sacrificial death. It helps us to see the true end of Jesus' lifelong mission. Through it, we understand that his suffering and death were not ends in themselves, but the necessary means for overcoming evil's stranglehold over the human heart.

Jesus' resurrection helps us to affirm our belief that love is stronger than death and that we have nothing to fear as our own earthly sojourn draws to a close. Jesus' resurrection completes the task of humanity's redemption and, in another sense, just begins it.

For his task to be fully over, the power of his redemptive suffering must be offered to every human heart. For that to happen, his message of plentiful redemption must not only be announced, but also lived. He has need of witnesses to his love who are also willing to suffer and, if need be, even die for the task which he has given them. Jesus has chosen to finish his work in and through us. He asks us to join him in leading others to the Father. He invites us to be his disciples and follow the path he has traveled.

Conclusion

"It is finished."

These words of Jesus from the cross speak of the end of his suffering and the completion of his mission. They are words of courage from someone intent on carrying out the Father's will, regardless of the consequences. They are words of expectant apprehension, enduring patience, and steadfast perseverance uttered at the end of a life violently cut short.

As he speaks the words, Jesus is about to breathe his last and release his spirit into his Father's hands. His mission is accomplished, yet only begun. There is always one more heart to open, one more spirit to move, one more soul to touch. As Jesus nears his end, he also approaches a beginning. After his death, it is his spirit, living in the hearts of his disciples, who will carry on his mission.

Jesus sees through his suffering and death in his final moments. Despite his deep physical agony and intense emotional pain, his trust in the Father has not been shaken. As he breathes his final breath, he calls upon the Father with hope and believes that love, not death, will be the final word. In his suffering and death, Jesus speaks a word of love to all humanity. That word springs from deep within his heart and, through the movement of his spirit, reaches out to every human heart that ever lived.

Jesus speaks words of heart from the heart. He directs them to no one and to everyone. Through them, he inspires his followers and silences his detractors. He also acknowledges the harsh reality of what is about to take place: Death draws near; darkness will soon encompass him. He will soon lie in the stillness of the grave.

The heart of the Father will mourn him in silence and then be moved to speak a word of life. With this life-giving word, the back of death will be broken—and all will be changed. In Jesus, God suffers and dies out of love for humanity. Because of his greatness of heart, humanity can now take heart. We can summon up the courage to face whatever comes. Because of Jesus' death, the reign of death has come to an end. Because of his resurrection, our new life of communion with God and each other has just barely begun.

Reflection Questions

1. What does it mean to be a person of heart? Does it have to do with sentimentality and passion or with courage, determination, and will? Was Jesus a person of heart? A person of courage? If so, why do you think this way? What evidence from his life makes you say so? Are you a person of heart? Of courage? Would you like to be? What evidence from your own life makes you say so?

2. Jesus had his eyes focused on his one and only end: doing the Father's will. Do you have your one and only end? If so, how would you describe it? Are you focused on it all of the time? What helps you to stay focused? What distracts you from your goal? Is your end in any way connected with Jesus? Have you ever looked to him for help?

3. What does it take to accomplish one's calling or task in life? Expectant apprehension? Enduring patience? Steadfast perseverance? A combination of all three? Can you think of any other qualities necessary for a person to fulfill his or her calling in life? Of all the qualities on your list, which are the more important? Which do you need the most?

4. Do you believe that Jesus' suffering and death continues to this day in the lives of the members of his body? If so, how do you envision this continuity? Is it real or simply metaphorical? How is your suffering a participation in that of Christ's? Is there any way in which it is not?

5. Even though you were not alive at the time, do you consider yourself a witness to Jesus' passion, death, and resurrection? If so, in what way? How do you give witness to it? How is this witness exemplified in your life? What more needs to be done? In what way is Jesus accomplishing his redemptive task in you? How are you passing his message on to others?

Prayer

Lord, I see you breathing your last and nearing death. I see you doing this for me, and I honestly do not know what to say. Lord, it is hard for me to imagine the depths of your love for me. It is difficult for me to understand how someone could be so selfless and giving of oneself. Lord, you stayed the course. You persevered until the very end. You not only lived, but also suffered and died so that humanity could once again turn to God. Lord, I thank you for your love. I thank you for your courage. I thank you for living and dying for me. Help me to become a worthy bearer of your love. Help me to stay the course, to remain faithful until the very end of my life. I know that I can do so only with your help. So help me, Lord, please help me. Mary, my mother, pray for me.

Chapter Seven
A Final Prayer

*"Father, into your hands
I commend my spirit."*

LUKE 23:46

In his last words from the cross, Jesus continues his prayer to the Father. In the midst of the Father's silence and an increasing sense of abandonment, Jesus keeps on trusting in the Father's love. His words from the cross echo the words of the psalmist: "Into your hands I commend my spirit; you will redeem me, LORD, faithful God" (Psalm 31:6). Jesus' final words are about redemption. He utters them as he faces the jaws of death and prays them on our behalf. We are the ones in need of redemption—not him.

Jesus is doing more, however, than merely recalling a verse from a well-known psalm. He has made these words his own, so much so that they cannot be fully understood without him. By taking on human flesh, the Word of God embraces the whole of humanity. Jesus is the new Adam, the one through whom sin is conquered and the reign of death overthrown. His final words from the cross represent an act of complete and total trust in the Father's care for him and for all humanity. There on Golgotha, the place of the skull, humanity is reborn through Jesus' baptism by fire. The waters of the Jordan, which he sanctified at the outset of his public ministry, flow from his side at the end of his life. Those same waters flow through the baptismal font and immerse us in his paschal mystery.

Jesus' final words let loose the streaming waters of Calvary and are, at one and the same time, both a song about humanity's hope for redemption and a simple, yet eloquent, sermon on the depths of God's love for us. Each of these words is rich with meaning and deserves reflection and careful scrutiny.

"Father." At the very end of his life, the psychological drama of Jesus' prayer from the cross has come full circle. His first words from his place of execution were addressed directly to his Father in heaven: "Father, forgive them, they know not what they do" (Luke 23:34). As time goes on, however, and as his suffering increases, he feels abandoned by the Father, so much so that he addresses him in a more traditional manner: "My God, my God, why have you forsaken me" (Matthew 27:46). Jesus, it seems, first interprets the Father's silence as abandonment. He feels alone in his sufferings and without the solace he has normally experienced in his relationship with the Father.

As his suffering grows, however, the depth of the Father's silence takes on deeper meaning for him. Jesus, whose trust never wavers, now embraces the Father's silence as the ultimate form of affirmation. As the Word of God made flesh and wisdom of the Father, he understands that the Father has no need to speak to him. He and the Father are one. If the Father is going to speak, it will come from Jesus' own lips. Jesus is the Word of the Father. There is no other.

Jesus' consolation comes only from doing the will of the Father. His desire to fulfill it leaves him hanging from the cross. The Father's will is still clear to him. Die he must for the sake of God's people. The cup of suffering has come to him, and he has accepted it. This full acceptance of the Father's will leads him to turn to the Father once more.

In his last words, he uses the intimate form of address that he had always been accustomed to using throughout his life: "Abba, Father." With these words, Jesus turns to the Father with loving affection. He understands the Father's silence as a strong yet quiet approval at what he has done for the sake of humanity.

The Gospel of Luke says Jesus uttered his last words in a loud voice (Luke 23:46). Some say that he did so to make his hearers understand that he was the true Son of God, calling God his Father. Others say that he did so to teach us that he did not die of necessity, but of his own free will.

Both interpretations are possible, as is a third: that he cried to his Father in a loud voice to reaffirm his trust in the Father's love. When seen in this light, Jesus, the true Son of God who gives himself over to death of his own accord, wishes to affirm once and for all that his Father has *not* abandoned him, but bathed him instead in the unfathomable depths of divine silence. From this womb of silence, the Father utters his Word of salvation to humanity. Against the backdrop of such silence, Jesus lived out his life on earth and offered his life on the cross for the life of the world. It was from such silence that Jesus himself was able to preach, to teach, and to heal. It was from such silence that death itself would soon be defeated and wonderfully overcome.

By addressing the Father in his very last words, Jesus emphasizes what is most important to him. Throughout his life, he lived for the glory of the Father. He wishes to make it exceptionally clear that he is doing so also in his death.

Jesus' life and death are intimately intertwined. We cannot understand his life apart from his death; nor can we fully appreciate his death apart from his life. We can understand neither apart from his relationship to the Father. That relationship gave him the strength to embrace his mission and carry it out. It enabled him to freely accept the cup of suffering that was placed before him—and without conditions. That relationship is what enabled him to trust in the Father's love for him, even when lost in the throes of complete and utter desolation. That relationship is what he wanted to share not only with his disciples, but also with the whole of humanity.

"Into your hands." Jesus' words to the Father have a clear direction and purpose. As we hear them, we imagine him looking to the hands that shaped the universe and all it contains. These hands are eternal and have always guided God's only begotten Son in his way. "God is love," we are told (1 John 4:8). As his breathes his last, Jesus looks to the Father's hands in order to be held and comforted by him. He has carried out the Father's will and, in releasing his spirit into his Father's hands, allows him to do with him as he would.

Jesus' last earthly act is to release his spirit into the Father's care. Through this action, Jesus expresses his deep love for the Father and his lasting trust in the Father's care. The Father's presence, we have seen, has manifested itself all during this time in silence.

Jesus commends his spirit into the silence of the Father's arms. There is nothing left to say. Jesus has said it all by his life and death.

The Gospels depict the earth and the heavens mourning Jesus' passage from life: "It was now about noon and darkness came over the whole land until three in the afternoon because of an eclipse of the sun. Then the veil of the temple was torn down the middle" (Luke 23:44–45). As Jesus commends his spirit into the Father's hands, we can nevertheless imagine the Father himself mourning through these ominous signs and wonders. The Father has remained silent throughout Jesus' passion.

At the moment of his Son's death, however, we should not be surprised that this silence would be broken. The Gospel of Matthew describes the scene in much more detail: "And behold, the veil of the sanctuary was torn in two from top to bottom. The earth quaked, rocks were split, tombs were opened, and the bodies of many saints who had fallen asleep were raised. And coming forth from their tombs after his resurrection, they entered the holy city and appeared to many. The centurion and the men with him who were keeping watch over Jesus feared greatly when they saw the earthquake and all that was happening, and they said, 'Truly, this was the Son of God!'" (Matthew 27:51–54). God the Father, the Creator of the universe, mourns the passing of his Son through a great display of power. More importantly than the earthquakes or the renting of the temple curtain or the raising of the saints from the dead, however, is the manifest spiritual power that could transform the cold, unbelieving hearts of the centurion and the men who were with him.

All of these are but a foreshadowing of what would be unleashed in three days. The stone would be rolled back. The shroud would be unwrapped and set aside. Jesus would open his eyes, be lifted up, and transformed. Many would experience him and come to believe in him. They would call him the Messiah, the Christ, the Anointed One. Countless more would believe on account of the testimony of these early witnesses. They would call him the Word of God, the Logos, the Father's Son. The story of Jesus' passion, death, and resurrection would be recounted again in small gatherings of believers around the table of the Lord where they all took part in the breaking of the bread.

The Father's hands that received Jesus' spirit at the moment of his death are the same hands that would raise him from the dead on Easter Sunday morning. They are strong, silent hands, hands of power and might, but also hands of consolation, joy, and compassion. It is fitting that just as the Father received Jesus' spirit at the moment of his death, his mother, Mary, would eventually receive his lifeless body into her hands when it was taken down from the cross. Jesus' Father and mother were present to him as he breathed his last. They are present to us at the last moment of our lives and receive our broken bodies and searching spirits into their loving hands.

"*I commend.*" Jesus' last words from the cross have not only purpose and direction, but also a great sense of release. Jesus took it upon himself to listen to the Father and to carry out his will. He suffered without complaint and of his own accord. He remained in control from beginning to end. No one could take this freedom from him. Jesus' last act before his death was to commit his spirit to his Father's care. This action was done freely and in trust. To place oneself in somebody's care means that one can no longer look out for oneself.

Jesus' last living action, however, was also greatly limited. Death was about to strip him of life. When he gives up his spirit, he will no longer be able to move or act in even the simplest of human ways. He will no longer be able to see or hear, to speak or smell or touch. Jesus knows what is about to happen and in his last human act delivers his spirit into his Father's care. True freedom, he knows, consists of doing the Father's will. With his end drawing near, Jesus understands where death is taking him. He commits himself to his Father's care, for he trusts the Father's love for him is stronger than the power of death. Jesus preserves his freedom by commending himself to the Father. No other hands would be able to handle what was to follow.

Jesus died a horrible death, but also a good death. The frightening dimensions of death by crucifixion need little explanation. It is one of the worst deaths imaginable. If given a choice of death, no one in his or her right mind would actively seek out this slow, tortuous means of separating the soul from the body. The Romans treated their animals—even those ready to be butchered—better than those they crucified. By all accounts, Jesus went through one of the most terrifying deaths possible. Perhaps part of the reason why so few went to the foot of the cross to witness his death was because the mere sight of his suffering was too horrible for them to bear.

At the same time, we can also see the reasons for saying why Jesus can be said to have died a good death. What better way to end one's life on earth than by talking to God and by expressly giving oneself into his care? Dying a good death means to be surrounded at the last moment of death with the necessary means for living in communion with God. Despite the appearances, Jesus' final moment of life on earth was blessed in this way. Jesus realized as he faced death that only one thing was necessary: to be in union with the Father. Jesus' final prayer to the Father was a heartfelt and endearing act of love. Jesus died a good death because he remained faithful to the Father until the very end. His good death was a fitting end to a good life, one lived in union with the Father and in solidarity with humanity's deepest desires.

What mattered most to Jesus, however, was not the manner in which he died or whether or not it could be said that he died a good death. What mattered most to him as he faced his final moments was if others would have access to the love he shared with the Father. Philosophers tell us that goodness is self-diffusive, that it cannot contain itself and must reach out to others. The divine plan of creation, redemption, and sanctification can be viewed as a corollary of this fundamental insight. The love of the triune God could not simply remain within itself for all eternity. Out of the freedom of this love, God chose to create us, to redeem us when we went astray, and to sanctify each one of us personally so that we could share in the intimate communion of divine love.

When seen in this light, Jesus' love for the Father always had an eye open for humanity. Just as the intersecting beams of the cross remind us of the close relationship between love of God and love of neighbor, we remember that Jesus' death on the cross was done out of love for both God and humanity. The will of the Father is intimately related to love of God and neighbor (see Matthew 22:37–39). Jesus embodied this love in life and in death. He asks his disciples, those who believe in him and seek to follow him, to do the same.

"My spirit." For the Jews of ancient Palestine, "spirit" was a person's life-breath. To lose it was to lose life itself. One could not survive without it. When Jesus commended his spirit to God, he was acknowledging the reality of his imminent death. Jesus' death involved the expiration of his spirit. As he breathed his last, he

let go of the life-breath that animated him and kept him alive. Jesus, we should remember, commends his human spirit into the Father's hands. It was his human spirit (not the Holy Spirit) that was exhausted and spent. Jesus was completely human in all respects: body, soul, and spirit. So was his death. He places his human spirit in the Father's care and, with it, that of all humanity.

At the same time, we must also recognize the close bond of communion between Jesus' human spirit and the Holy Spirit. Humanity's hope of unity with the Father lies in this close, intimate bond which took shape at the Incarnation and was baptized in the blood of Jesus' passion and death. Although a clear distinction exists between Jesus' human spirit and his Holy Spirit, the close bond of solidarity between them implies that both had left him at the hour of his death: the human one by way of necessity; the divine, because of the Father's will. Jesus' experience of abandonment by the Father, in other words, also extended to the Spirit.

Moments before his death, he cried out: "My God, my God, why have you forsaken me?" (Matthew 27:46). The term "God," in this context, is taken to refer to both the Father and the Spirit. No one is there to comfort him, not even the Divine Comforter. On a still deeper level, however, Jesus knew that both the Father and the Spirit were silently present to him in the midst of his suffering and death. Nevertheless, Jesus feels forsaken by both the Father and the Spirit in his moment of extreme agony.

At the moment of his death, he loudly reaffirms his deep, lasting, and unshaken trust in the Father and commends both his human spirit and the Holy Spirit to his care. For Jesus, the two were so closely united that they were perceived and acted upon as one.

Finally, when Jesus commends his spirit to the Father, he offers along with it the spirit of all humanity. In his final act of earthly freedom, he entrusts the human spirit—the vitality and lifeblood of the human race—to the Father's care. This act was something we could not do of our own accord. Someone had to do it for us, someone like us but also like God, someone human but also divine. In this final act, Jesus acts as the true mediator between God and man. He takes our place before God and intercedes for us. In his last words, he prays the prayer we longed to pray but could not. He takes us with him as he faces death and places us with him in the Father's care. We face death together, and, because we are in the Father's care, together we shall overcome it. Jesus has identified himself so closely with humanity that his story has become our story, and our story, his. Because of this close identity, we trust that he who suffered and died for us will be there for us in our time of need. Jesus identifies our needs with his needs. Anything we ask the Father in his name, we shall receive (see John 15:16).

Conclusion

"Father, into your hands I commend my spirit."

Jesus' final words from the cross are a prayer from the heart addressed to "Abba," his Father in heaven. Jesus' Father is also our Father. We, too, are encouraged to turn to him with deep, heartfelt prayers in times of need, especially at our hour of death. We should not hesitate to do so and need not be afraid. Jesus has already spoken to him on our behalf: he has carried us in his heart and given it to his Father; he asks us to open our hearts and do the same.

The Father's hands are silent and strong, loving and compassionate. They are ready to receive us whenever we are ready to offer ourselves to him and entrust our spirits to his care. He asks us only to allow him to be God in our lives so that he can also be God for us in our deaths. Jesus lived and died in this way—and so should we. We do so by opening our hearts to the Father. Such prayer goes a long way. Jesus' last words from the cross show this to be so.

With our hearts in the Father's care, we have nothing to fear. With Jesus, we, too, can cry out in a loud voice to give witness to the Father's love for us. As the Apostle Paul reminds us: "… neither death, nor life, nor angels, nor principalities, nor present things, nor future things, nor powers, nor height, nor depth, nor any other creature will be able to separate us from the love of God in Christ Jesus our Lord" (Romans 8:38–39). Through his life, death, and resurrection, Jesus has brought us back to the Father's love. Because of him, nothing can separate us from that love. As with Jesus, our last words on earth should express a deep, lasting trust in the Father; we, too, should commend our spirits to his care. Wherever we are, the Father's hands will always be waiting for us. A special place is reserved for each of us—in the palm of his hand.

Reflection Questions

1. Do you trust God to save you? Do you trust him above all things, even when he seems distant and far away? Do you pray to him even when he does not seem to respond? Do you trust him with your life? Your death? Your family and friends? How can you trust him more?

2. How do you normally react to silence? Does it make you feel uncomfortable? Unsettled? Afraid? How do you react to the silence that accompanies extended periods of prayer? Does it make you feel distracted? Lonely? Uncared for? Abandoned? Have you learned how to listen to the silence within your heart? Have you learned how to interpret this silence? Have you learned how to turn this silence into solitude?

3. Was Jesus free during his death—or limited? In what ways was he free? In what ways was he limited? Did Jesus liberate humanity by voluntarily limiting himself? Is this self-limitation a part of the logic of selfless love? Have you ever experienced something similar in your own life? Can you think of concrete examples from your life where this proved to be so?

4. How do you see the relationship between the love of God and the love of neighbor? Are they one and the same? Completely separate? Closely connected? Does Jesus' suffering and death on the cross tell you anything about the relationship between the two? Does his resurrection? What does God's love for you

tell you about your love for God? Does it tell you anything about your love for your neighbor? Should it?

5. How do you view the relationship between the Holy Spirit and your own spirit? Are they one and the same? Completely distinct? Do they communicate in any way? Do they commune with one another? Does Jesus' death and resurrection have anything to do with your understanding of this relationship? How do you listen to the spirit in your life? Do you know when you are not listening? How can you tell the difference?

Prayer

~~~~~~~~~~~~

Lord, I see you crying out in a loud voice and commending your spirit into your Father's hands. With those words, I also see you doing the same for all of humanity. Seeing you die brings me no comfort, Lord. It was so slow and horrible. It pains me to think of what you went through. It saddens me to see how little we appreciate your love for us. Lord, help me to unite my voice with yours. Help me demonstrate my love for you through my thoughts, words, and actions. Help me to entrust my life to the Father's care. Lord, fill me with your Holy Spirit and help me to live and to die with you and for you. Your love is all that is needed, Lord. In my living, my dying, and my rising, it is the one thing necessary. Mary, my mother, woman of love, pray for me.

The Triumph of the Cross

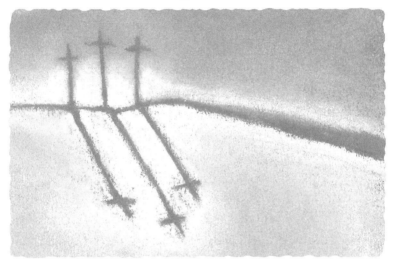

Jesus' last words from the cross fill us with awe at the depths of his love for God and humanity. He emptied himself to be filled with our humanity and offered himself to his Father in our place. The cross was the means by which he demonstrated the extent of his love. He was not intimidated by its brutality or frightened by its deadly grasp. He faced his executioners with hopeful resignation; his imminent end with quiet resolve. The cross brought Jesus to the threshold of death. Through it, he experienced the full impact of humanity's willful separation from God.

Jesus identified with us so closely that he bore on his shoulders the full weight of our human sinfulness. His innocence replaced our guilt. Jesus entered our world not to condemn it, but to save it (see John 3:17). He did so by embracing death on our behalf so that our destiny could be inexorably bound up with his. His destiny was to live and die by the power of love, a force he unleashed on the world through his suffering and death on the cross.

Jesus defeated the power of death with the powerlessness of love. Although death had embraced Jesus by imprinting its cold, lifeless marks into his bloodied limbs and *corpus*, it could not subdue him, for he had overcome his fear of death and commended his spirit to his Father's care. That care would become our hope and the cause of our salvation. It would bind up our wounds and heal our hearts. It would bring us back to health and lead us to new life. It would show us the way to the kingdom and enable us, with Jesus, to share in the riches of the Father's glory.

The triumph of the cross demonstrates the power of God's love for humanity. It celebrates Jesus' victory over death and marks a decisive defeat over evil's power to hold sway in our hearts. Just as Moses in the desert raised the serpent on a pole to heal all who cast their eyes upon it from the venomous poison within them (see Numbers 21:4–9), so was Jesus lifted up on the wood of the cross to bring eternal life to all who look to him in faith (see John 3:14–15). Wandering through the desert with poison in one's veins is an apt description of the human situation. Moses gained healing for his people by interceding to God on their behalf. Jesus does the same and gains healing for us not from a single encounter with venomous snakes, but from death itself. Because of Jesus' death on the cross, the deadly poison flowing in our veins has been extracted; the antidote generously applied. On the wood of the cross, the selflessness of love struggled with the power of death—and proved victorious.

In the end, Jesus' last words from the cross were not his final ones. Through the empty tomb of Easter morning, he spoke more eloquently still. After the stone was rolled back, some of his first words to his disciples were, "Peace be with you," and "Do not be afraid" (see Matthew 28:9–10; Luke 24:36; John 20:19, 21, 26). Centuries later, Jesus addresses these same words to us, offering us the peace of his kingdom and the love of God living in our hearts. He invites us to follow him in preaching his message of peace. He bids us to be bold and courageous. He asks us not to count the cost. There is nothing to fear, he promises us, for he has turned the cross from a weapon of death into an instrument of love. Because of him, death has relinquished its power; it has lost its sting. We have been set free by the powers of the Lord's death and resurrection. We have the sign and assurance of the triumph of the cross. The words of Saint Paul lift high the standard and remind us of the road ahead: "Thanks be to God who gives us the victory through our Lord Jesus Christ. Therefore, my beloved brothers, be firm, steadfast, always fully devoted to the work of the Lord, knowing that in the Lord your labor is not in vain" (1 Corinthians 15:57–58).

Jesus' victory is our victory; his triumph on the cross, a triumph for the human heart. Whenever we look at the wood of the cross, let us remember Jesus' last words as he hung from it. May they be engraved in our hearts. May they inspire us to love others as he loved us. May they help us to give of ourselves as he gave of himself. May they ever remind us of the great price paid for our redemption and help us to understand that, as members of his body, we continue to pay that price today. The drama of the cross continues to this day, enacted in our lives and living in our hearts. Jesus still speaks to us of his kingdom of love. He asks us to listen both to his words and to the silence that makes them possible. He asks us to seek him in our hearts and to share what we discover there with those around us.

Resurrection

Something strange is happening.
There is a great silence on earth today,
a great silence and stillness.
The whole earth keeps silence
because the King is asleep.

The earth trembled and is still,
because God has fallen asleep in the flesh,
and he has raised up all who have slept
ever since the world began.

God has died in the flesh,
and hell trembles with fear.

. . .

[Christ spoke to Adam:]

"I order you, O sleeper, to awake.

I did not create you to be held a prisoner in hell.
Rise from the dead,
for I am the life of the dead.
Rise up, work of my hands,
you who were created in my image.
Rise, let us leave this place,
for you are in me
and I am in you.
Together we form only one person
and we cannot be separated.

—FROM AN ANCIENT HOMILY

Notes

About the Author

Dennis J. Billy, CSsR, a Redemptorist of the Baltimore Province, holds a ThD in church history from Harvard Divinity School, an STD in spirituality from the Pontifical University of Saint Thomas, and a DMin in spiritual direction from the Graduate Theological Foundation. He was professor of the history of moral theology and Christian spirituality at the Alphonsian Academy of Rome's Pontifical Lateran University for more than 20 years and is currently the John Cardinal Krol Chair of Moral Theology at Saint Charles Borromeo Seminary, Overbrook, in Wynnewood, Pennsylvania. He has written more than 25 books and has published more than 300 articles in a number of well-known scholarly and popular journals.

Other Related
Liguori Publications Titles...

Blessings of the Rosary
Meditations on the Mysteries
Dennis J. Billy, CSsR
ISBN: 978-0-7648-1941-4

Offering prayerful reflections on each of the twenty mysteries of the rosary along with thoughtful questions that will inspire a richer awareness of God's presence. The reflections in *Blessings of the Rosary* will encourage readers to make the rosary an integral part of their daily devotions. These reflections will be of immeasurable spiritual benefit to individuals and groups engaged in the crucial work of prayer.

The Women of the Passion
Kathleen M. Murphy
ISBN: 978-0-7648-1647-5

These reflections unravel the stories of women who accompanied Jesus during his last days and were there as he endured his agony and death on the cross. Each reflection is well-researched, yet easily readable and thought-provoking. They show how much we know about these women and what they have to share. Each chapter ends with questions that will help the reader be open to experience the healing, the mercy, and the compassion of Christ that comes from the knowledge of the risen Jesus.

Lent and Easter Wisdom From St. Benedict
Judith Sutera, OSB
ISBN: 978-0-7648-1968-1

Lent and Easter Wisdom From St. Ignatius of Loyola
The Maryland Province of the Society of Jesus
ISBN: 978-0-7648-1821-9

For prices and ordering information, call us toll free at 800-325-9521 or visit our Web site, www.liguori.org.